THE DEADLY

BELL WITCH GHOST

A GHOSTLY GRAPHIC

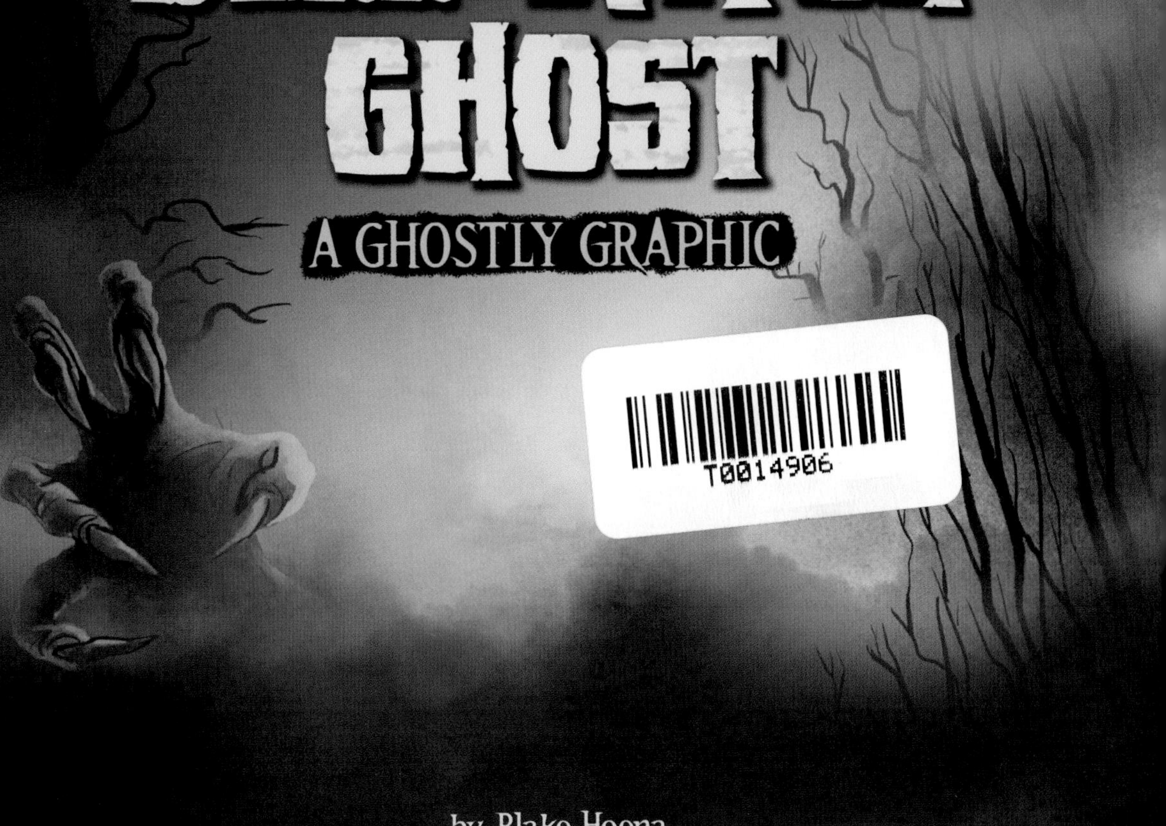

by Blake Hoena
illustrated by Amerigo Pinelli

CAPSTONE PRESS
a capstone imprint

Published by Capstone Press, an imprint of Capstone
1710 Roe Crest Drive, North Mankato, Minnesota 56003
capstonepub.com

Library of Congress Cataloging-in-Publication Data is available
on the Library of Congress website.

ISBN: 9781669050667 (hardcover)
ISBN: 9781669071303 (paperback)
ISBN: 9781669050629 (ebook PDF)

Summary: In 1817, a terrifying specter began haunting John Bell and his
family in Tennessee. At first, the spooky spirit's knocking and scratching
sounds seemed harmless. But soon, the phantom's antics became more
sinister—and even deadly! Who was the Bell Witch? And why did she
torment John and his family?

Editorial Credits
Editor: Christopher Harbo; Designer: Tracy Davies;
Production Specialist: Katy LaVigne

All internet sites appearing in back matter were available
and accurate when this book was sent to press.

Printed and bound in the USA. 5425

TABLE OF CONTENTS

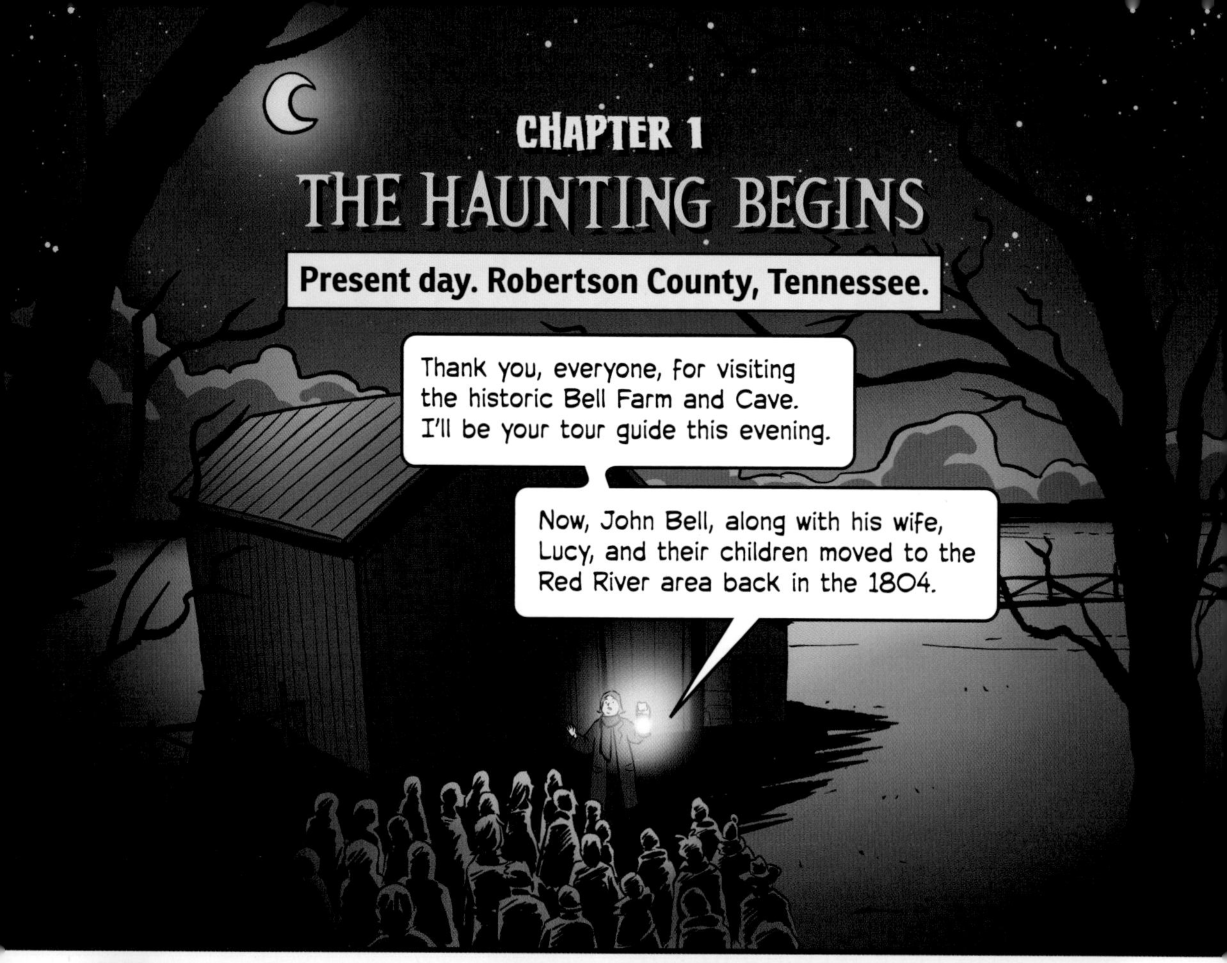
CHAPTER 1
THE HAUNTING BEGINS
Present day. Robertson County, Tennessee.
Thank you, everyone, for visiting the historic Bell Farm and Cave. I'll be your tour guide this evening.
Now, John Bell, along with his wife, Lucy, and their children moved to the Red River area back in the 1804.

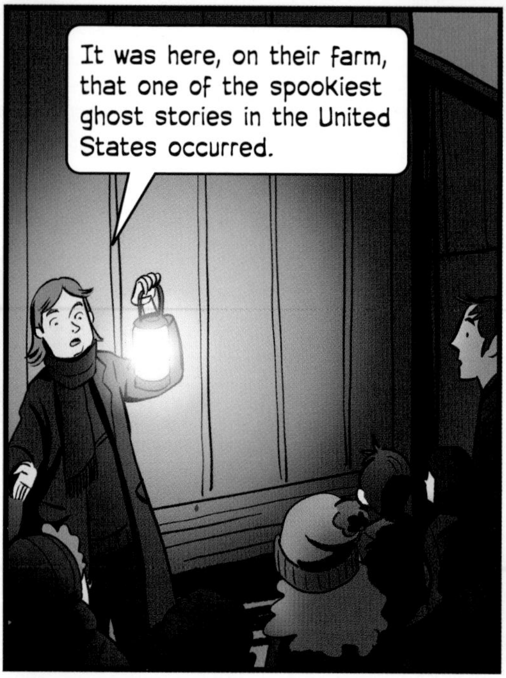
It was here, on their farm, that one of the spookiest ghost stories in the United States occurred.

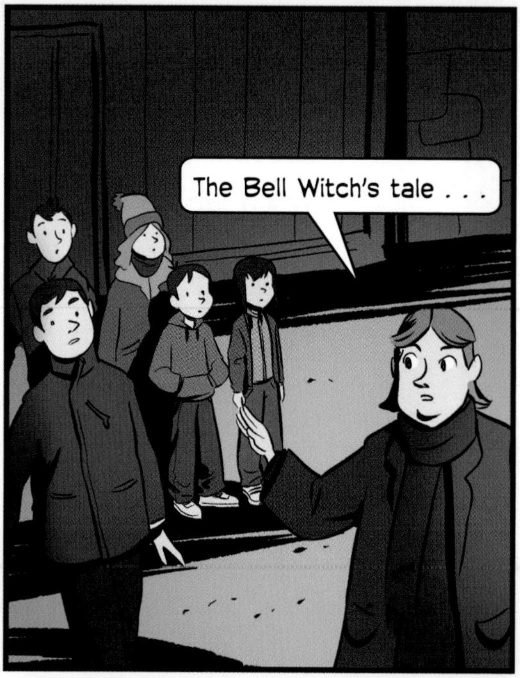
The Bell Witch's tale . . .

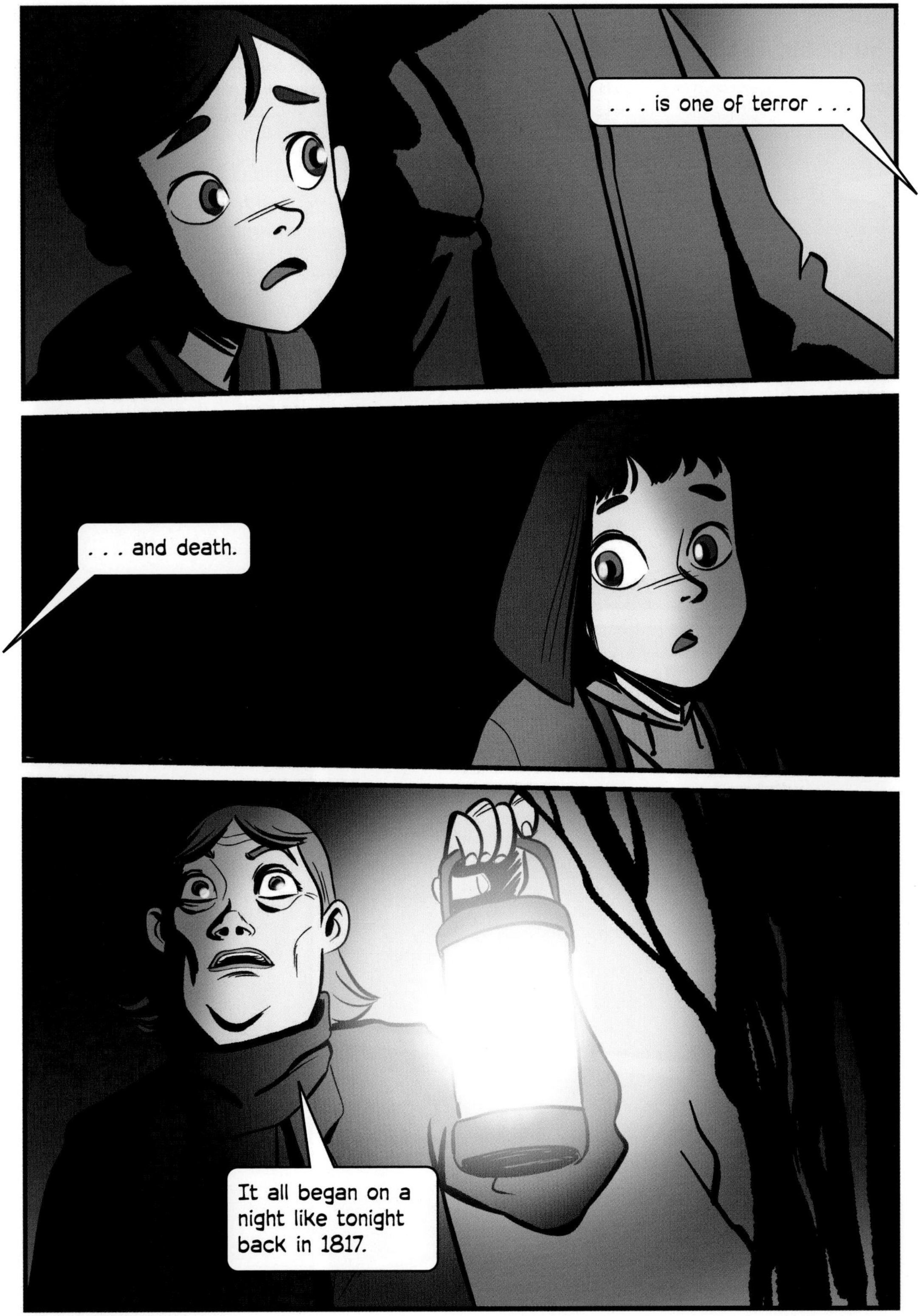
. . . is one of terror . . .
. . . and death.
It all began on a night like tonight back in 1817.

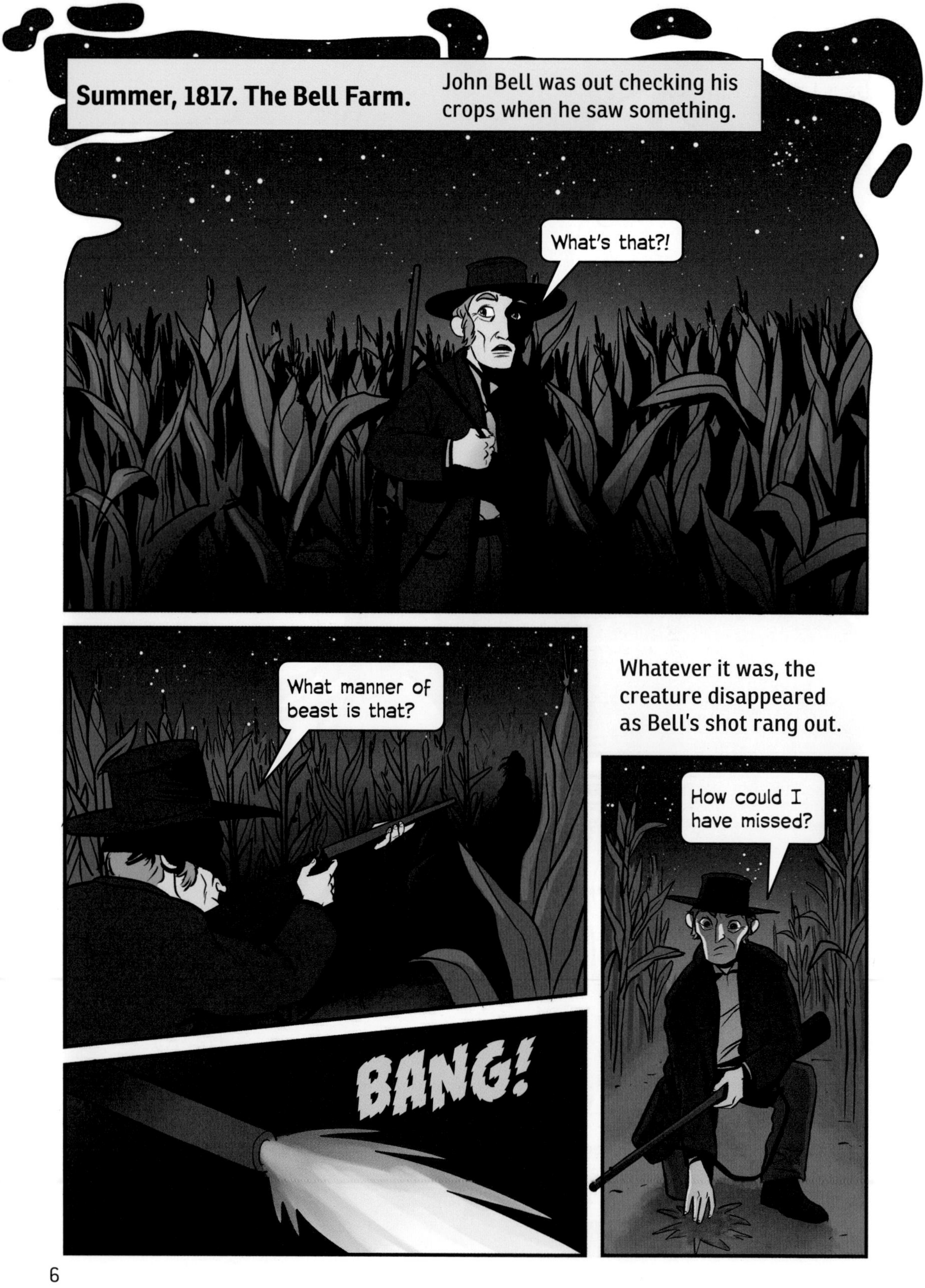
Summer, 1817. The Bell Farm.
John Bell was out checking his crops when he saw something.
What's that?!
What manner of beast is that?
BANG!
Whatever it was, the creature disappeared as Bell's shot rang out.
How could I have missed?

Days later, John's son Drew went out for a walk.

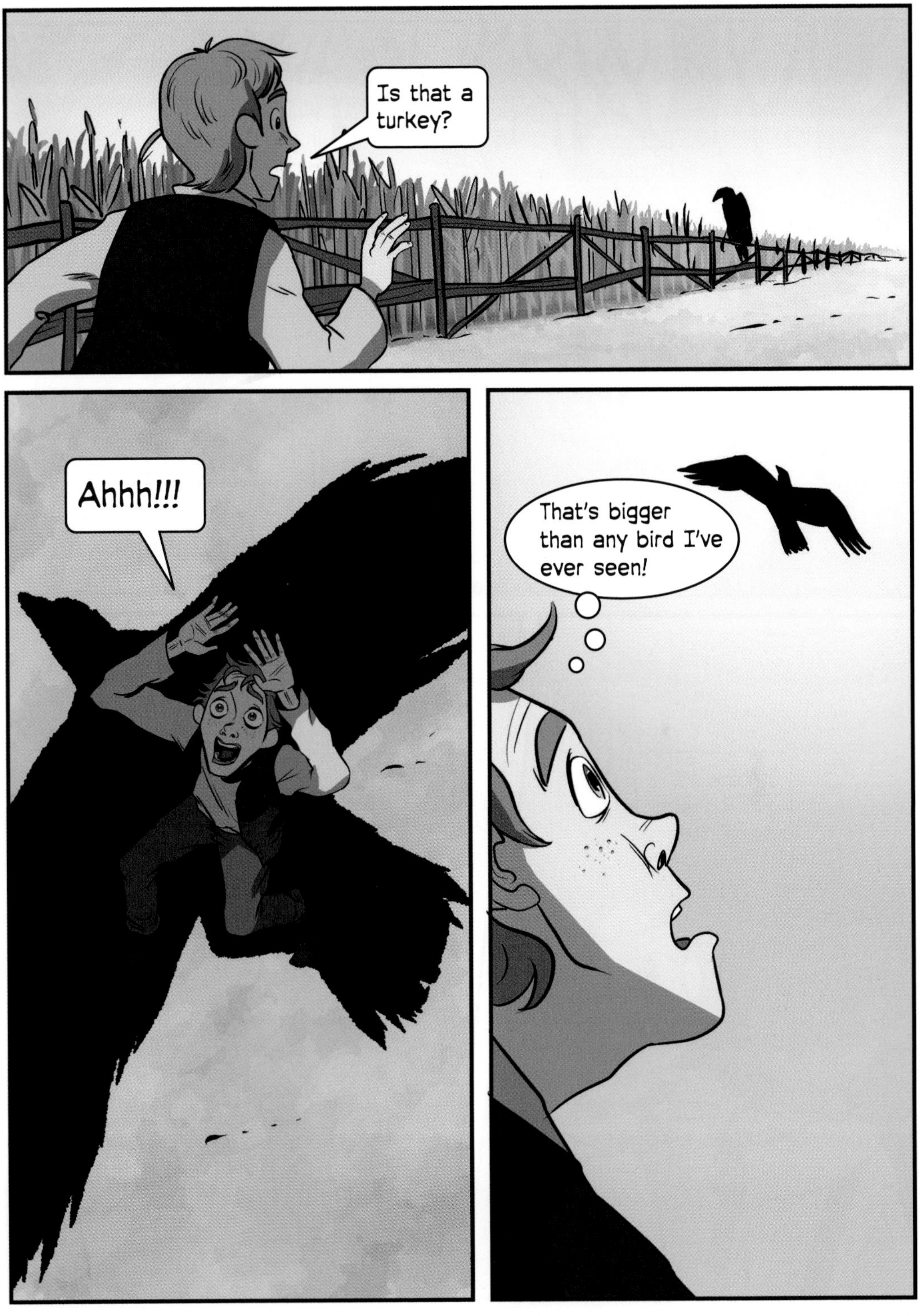
Is that a turkey?
Ahhh!!!
That's bigger than any bird I've ever seen!

The Bell family continued to see strange things around their farm.

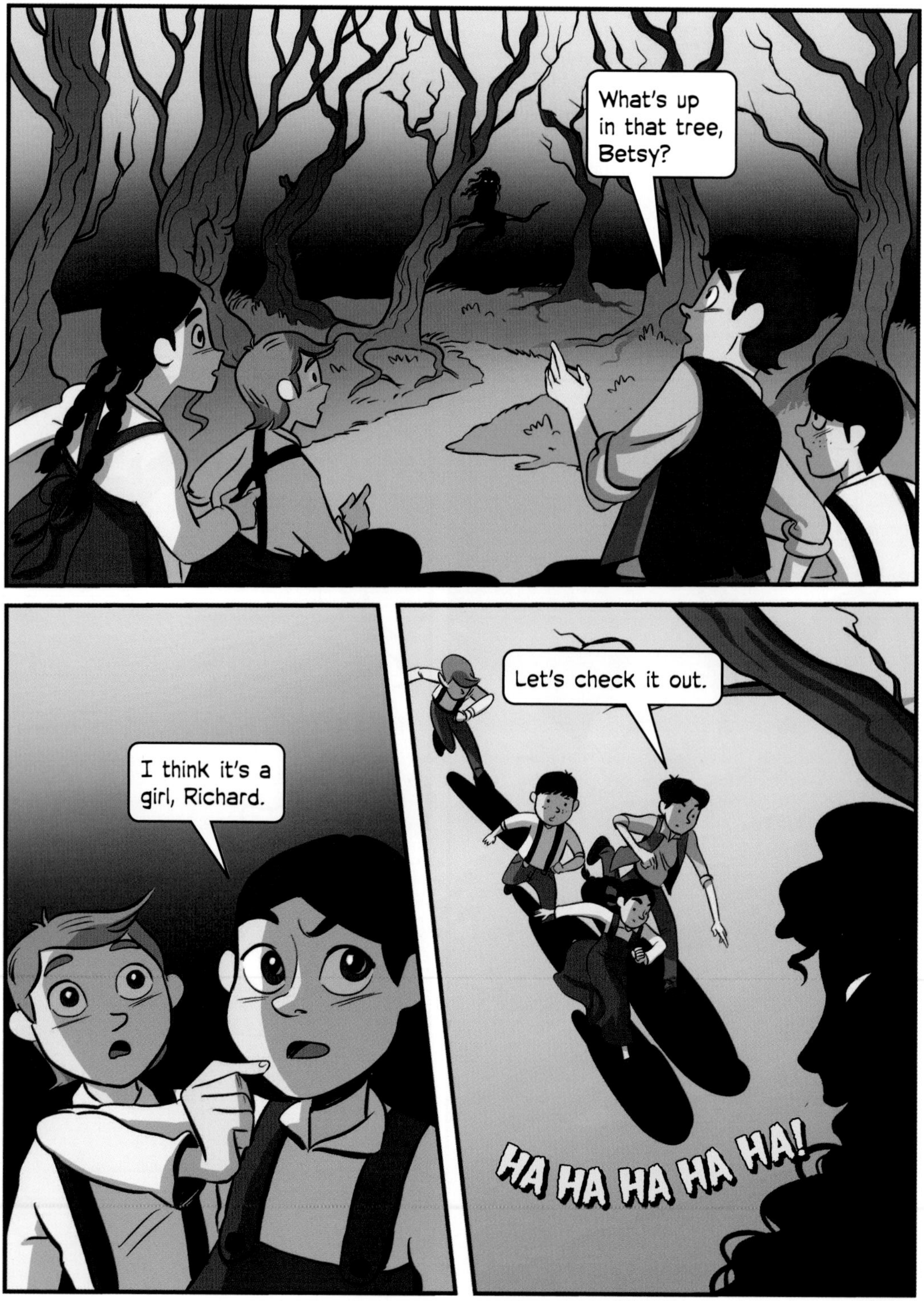
What's up in that tree, Betsy?
I think it's a girl, Richard.
Let's check it out.
HA HA HA HA HA HA!

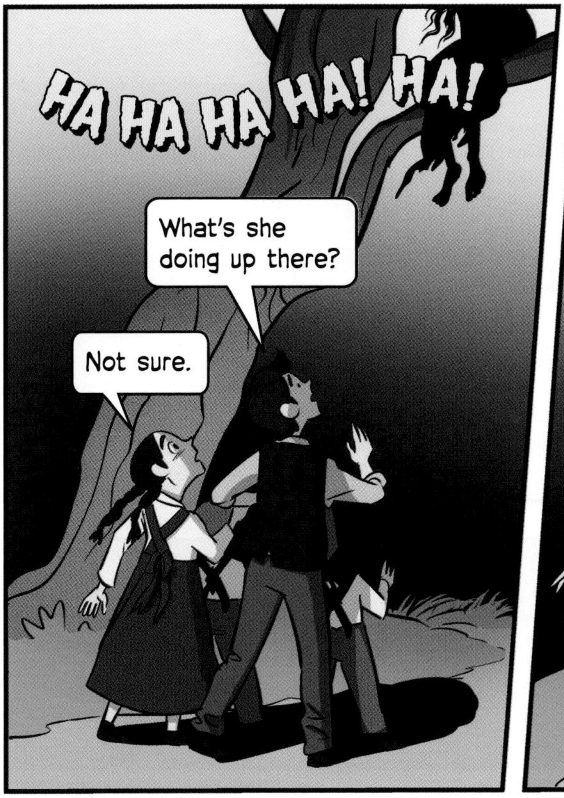
HA HA HA HA! HA!
What's she doing up there?
Not sure.

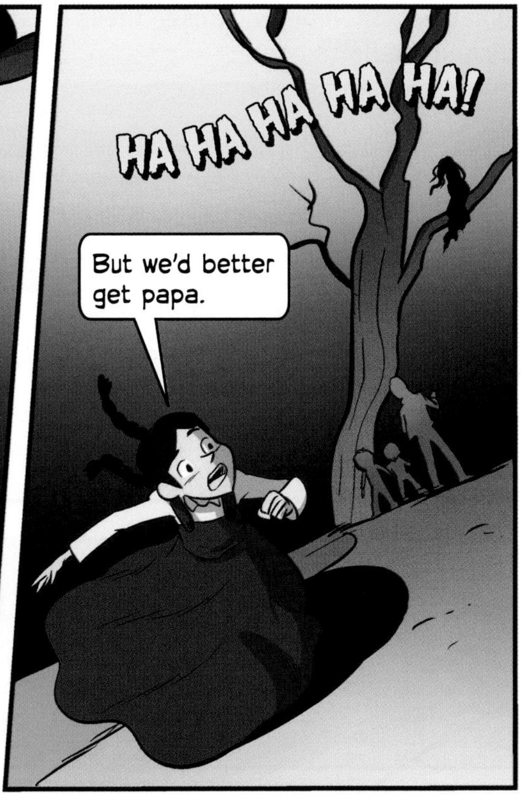
HA HA HA HA HA!
But we'd better get papa.

But when they returned . . .

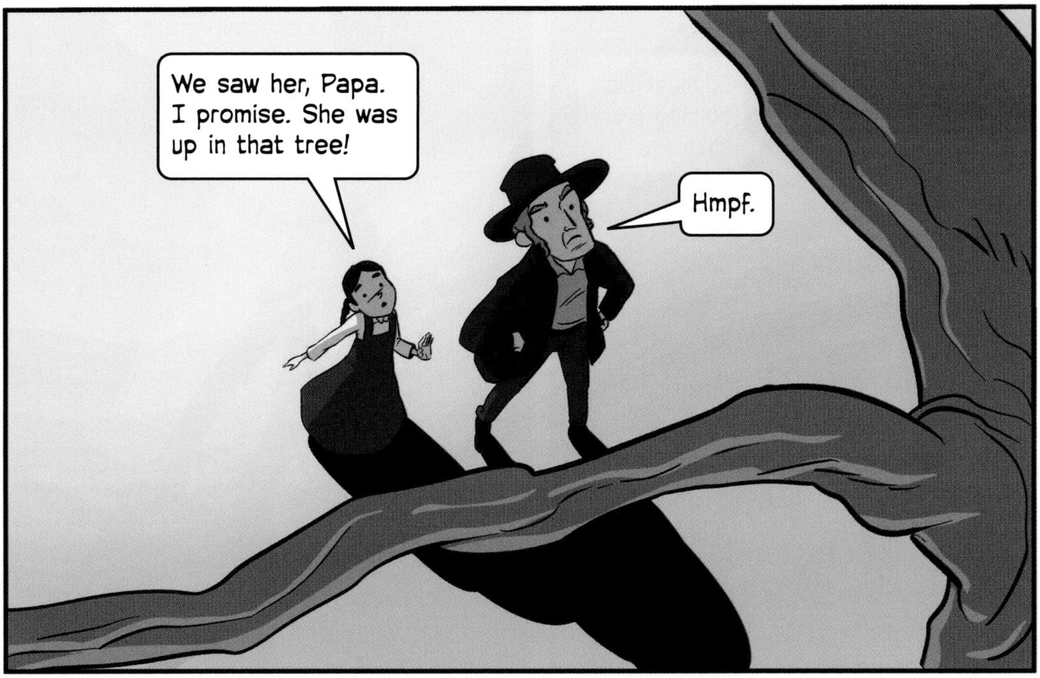
We saw her, Papa. I promise. She was up in that tree!
Hmpf.

Whatever, or whoever, caused these mysterious events soon visited the Bell's home.

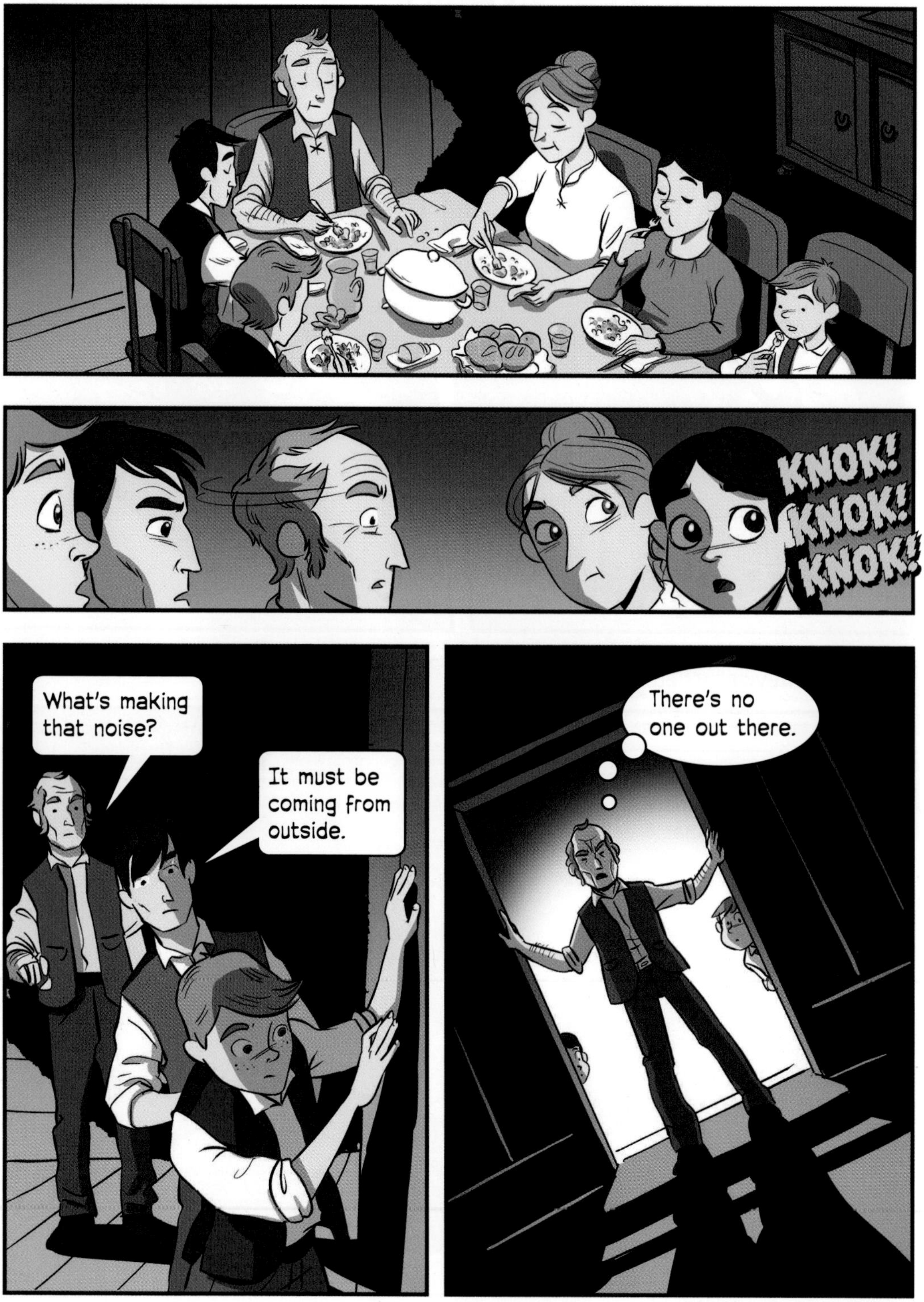
KNOK! KNOK! KNOK!
What's making that noise?
It must be coming from outside.
There's no one out there.

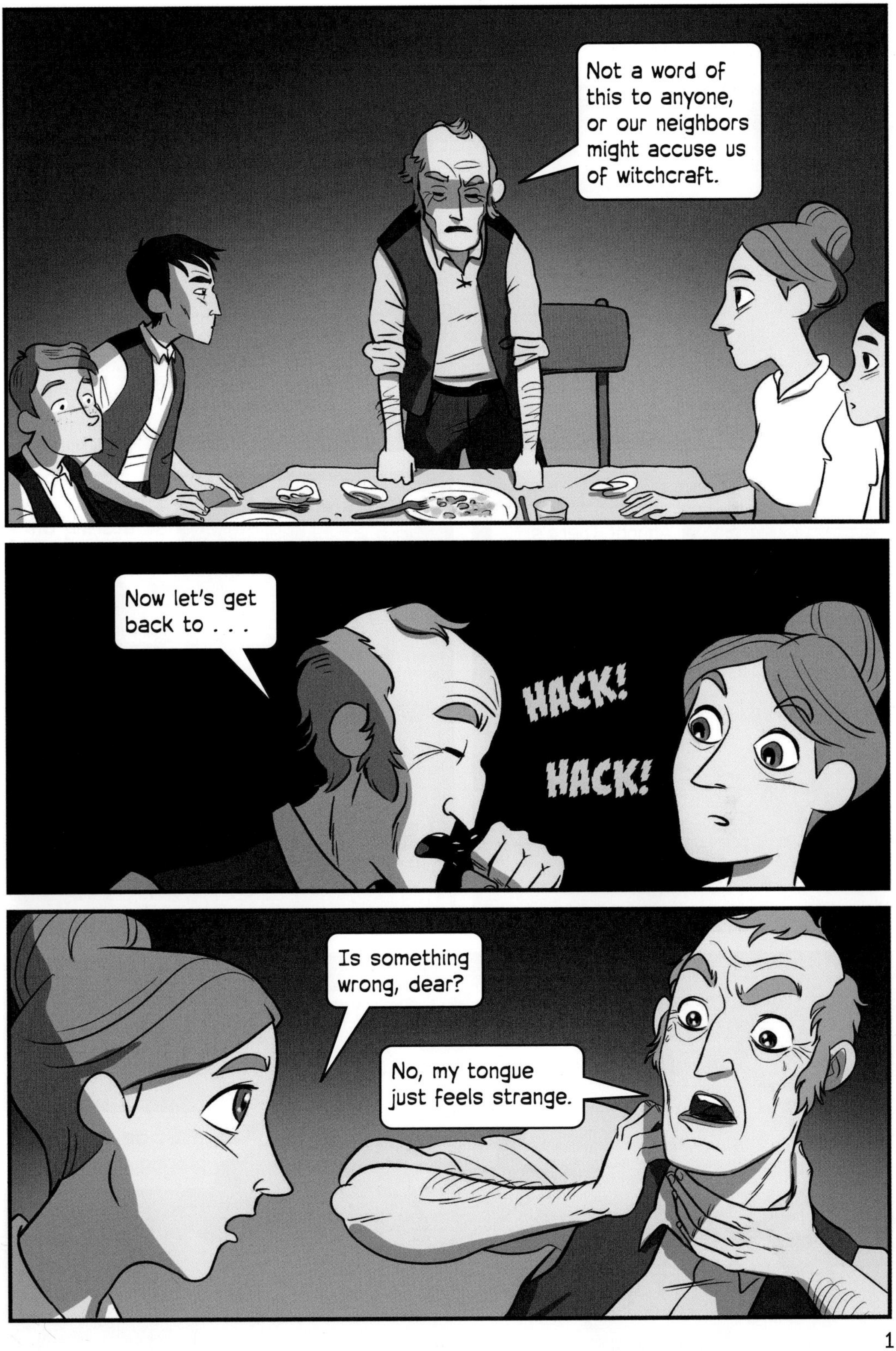
Not a word of this to anyone, or our neighbors might accuse us of witchcraft.
Now let's get back to . . .
HACK!
HACK!
Is something wrong, dear?
No, my tongue just feels strange.

While John Bell had sworn his family to secrecy, the Bell Witch was just getting started.

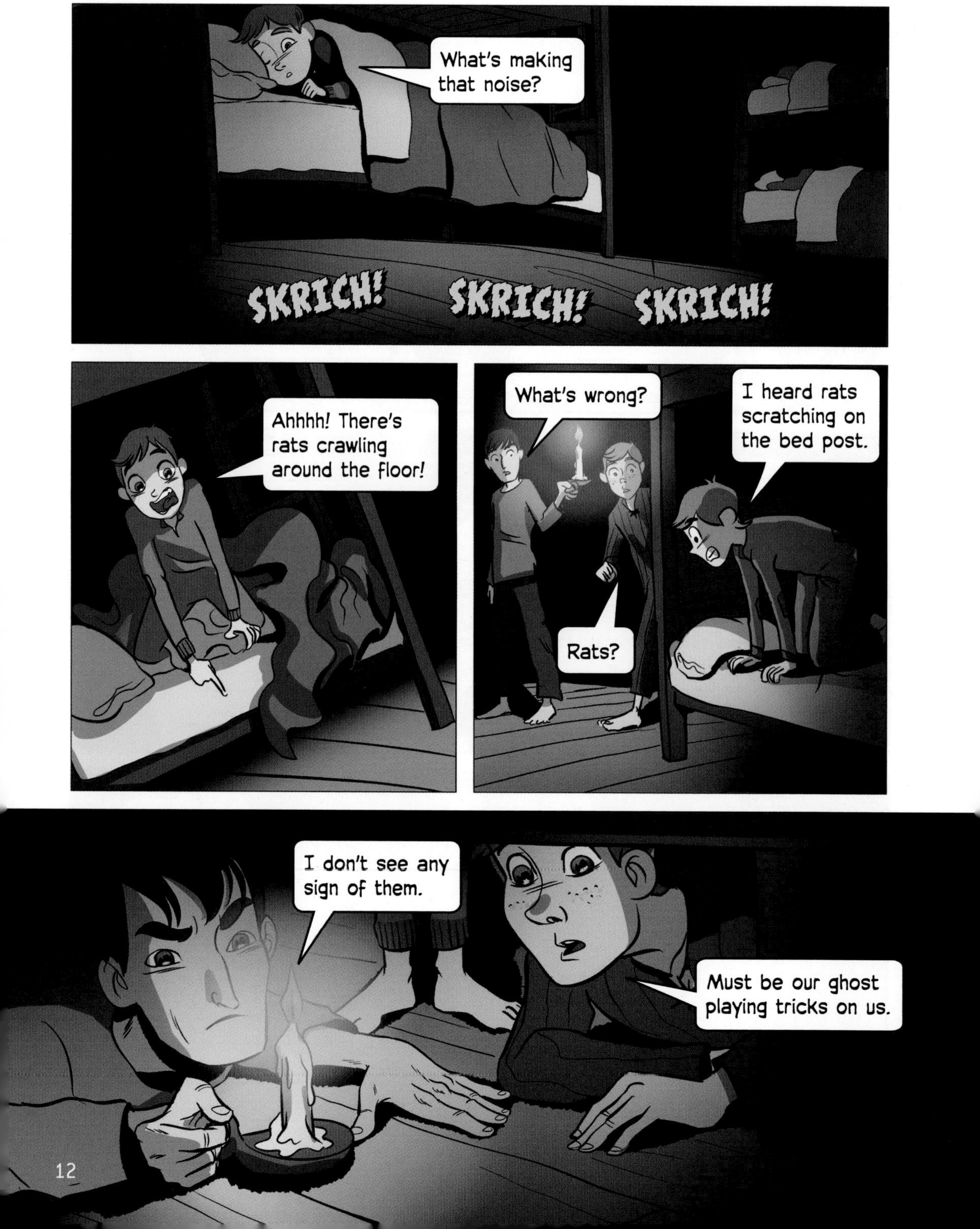
What's making that noise?
SKRICH! SKRICH! SKRICH!
Ahhhh! There's rats crawling around the floor!
What's wrong?
Rats?
I heard rats scratching on the bed post.
I don't see any sign of them.
Must be our ghost playing tricks on us.

All sorts of strange noises haunted the Bells, but that wasn't the worst of it.

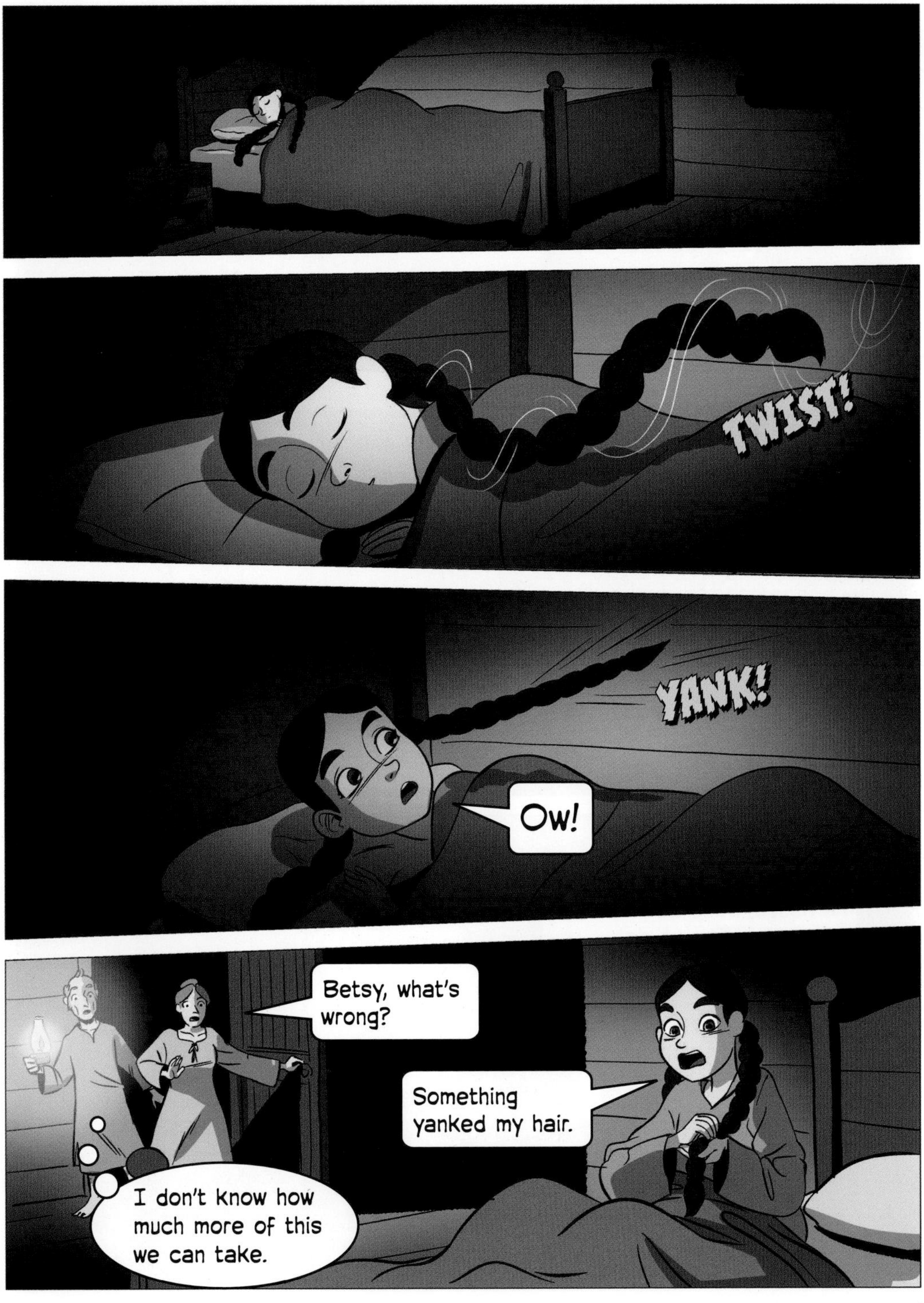
TWIST!
YANK!
Ow!
Betsy, what's wrong?
Something yanked my hair.
I don't know how much more of this we can take.

CHAPTER 2

THE BELL WITCH SPEAKS

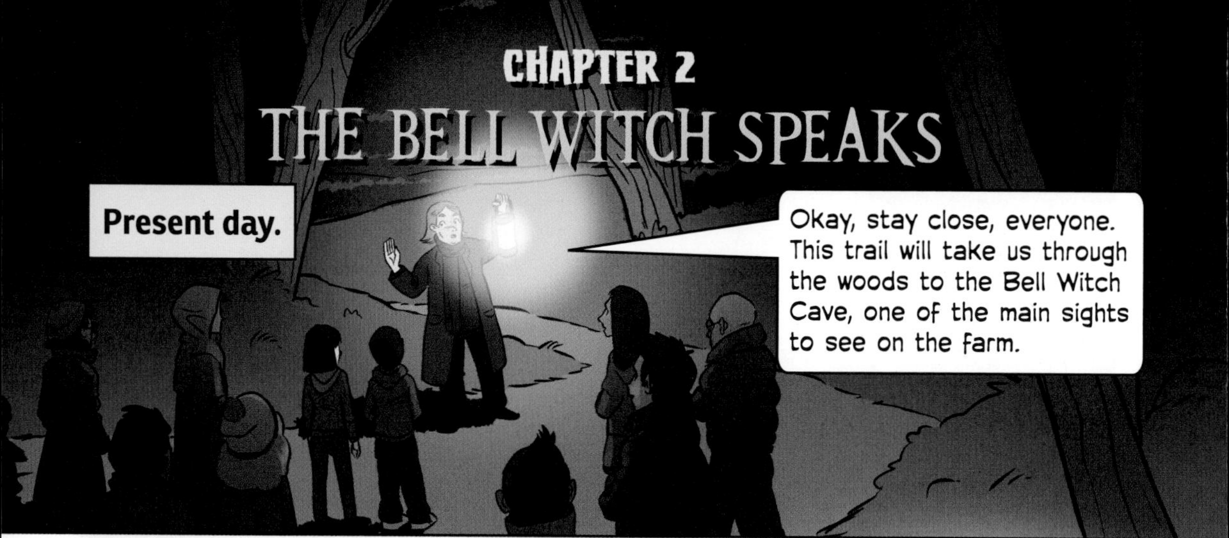

Present day.
Okay, stay close, everyone. This trail will take us through the woods to the Bell Witch Cave, one of the main sights to see on the farm.

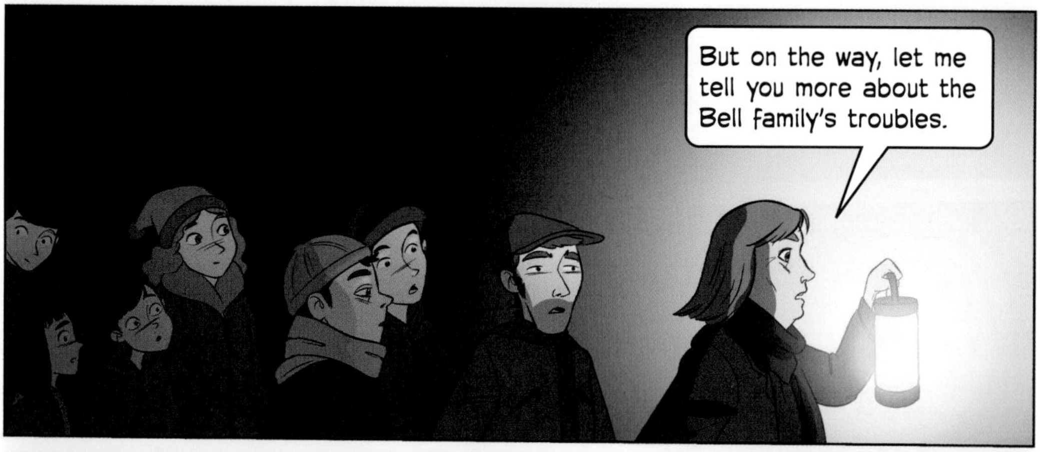

But on the way, let me tell you more about the Bell family's troubles.

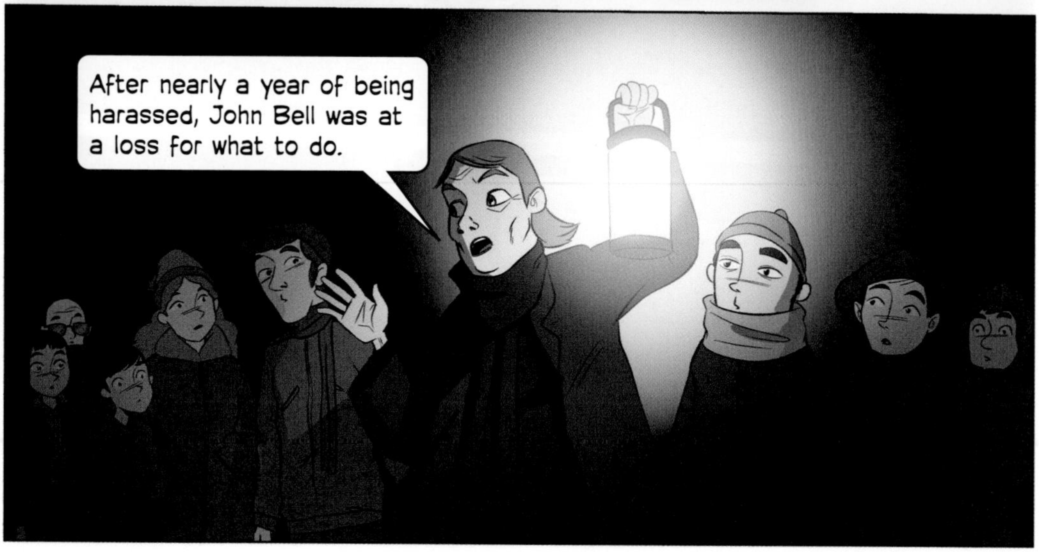

After nearly a year of being harassed, John Bell was at a loss for what to do.

Summer, 1818. The Bell Farm.

So he asked his neighbor, Mr. James Johnson, for help.

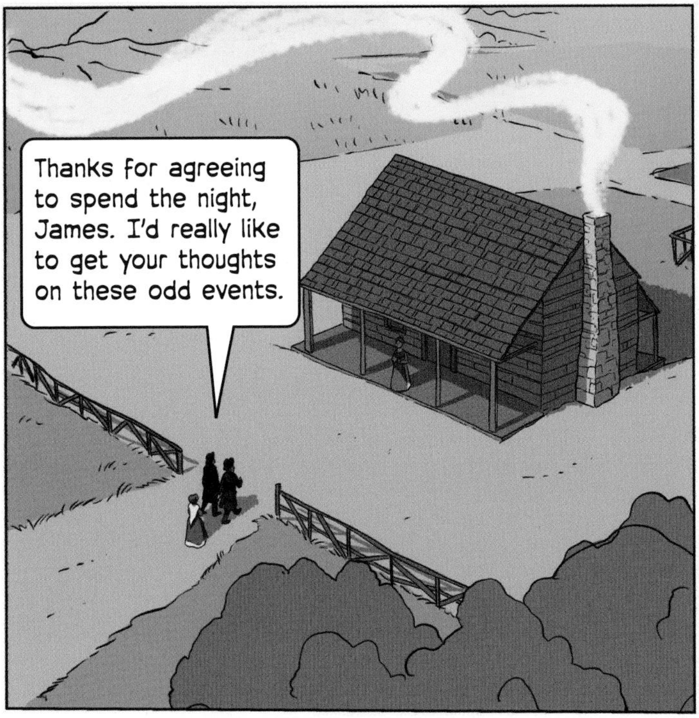
Thanks for agreeing to spend the night, James. I'd really like to get your thoughts on these odd events.

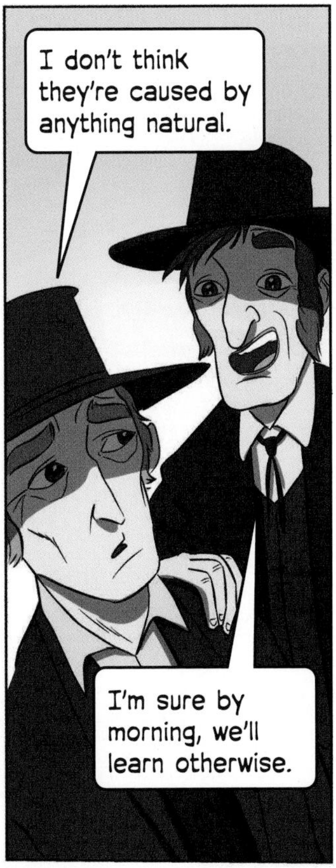
I don't think they're caused by anything natural.
I'm sure by morning, we'll learn otherwise.

Before going to bed that night, Mr. Johnson led everyone in prayer.

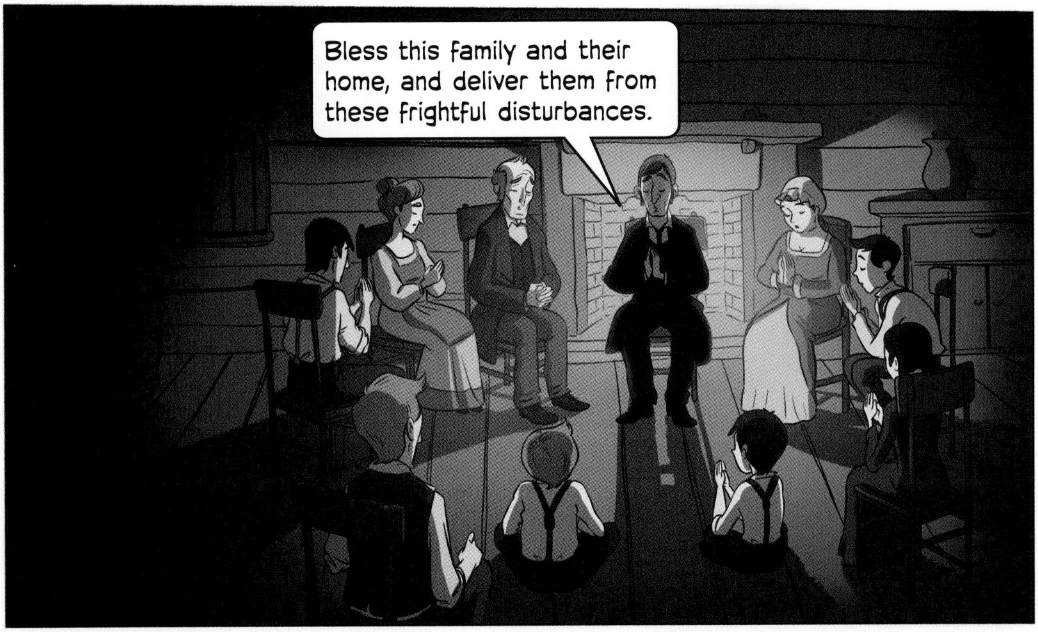
Bless this family and their home, and deliver them from these frightful disturbances.

But not long after everyone was tucked into bed . . .

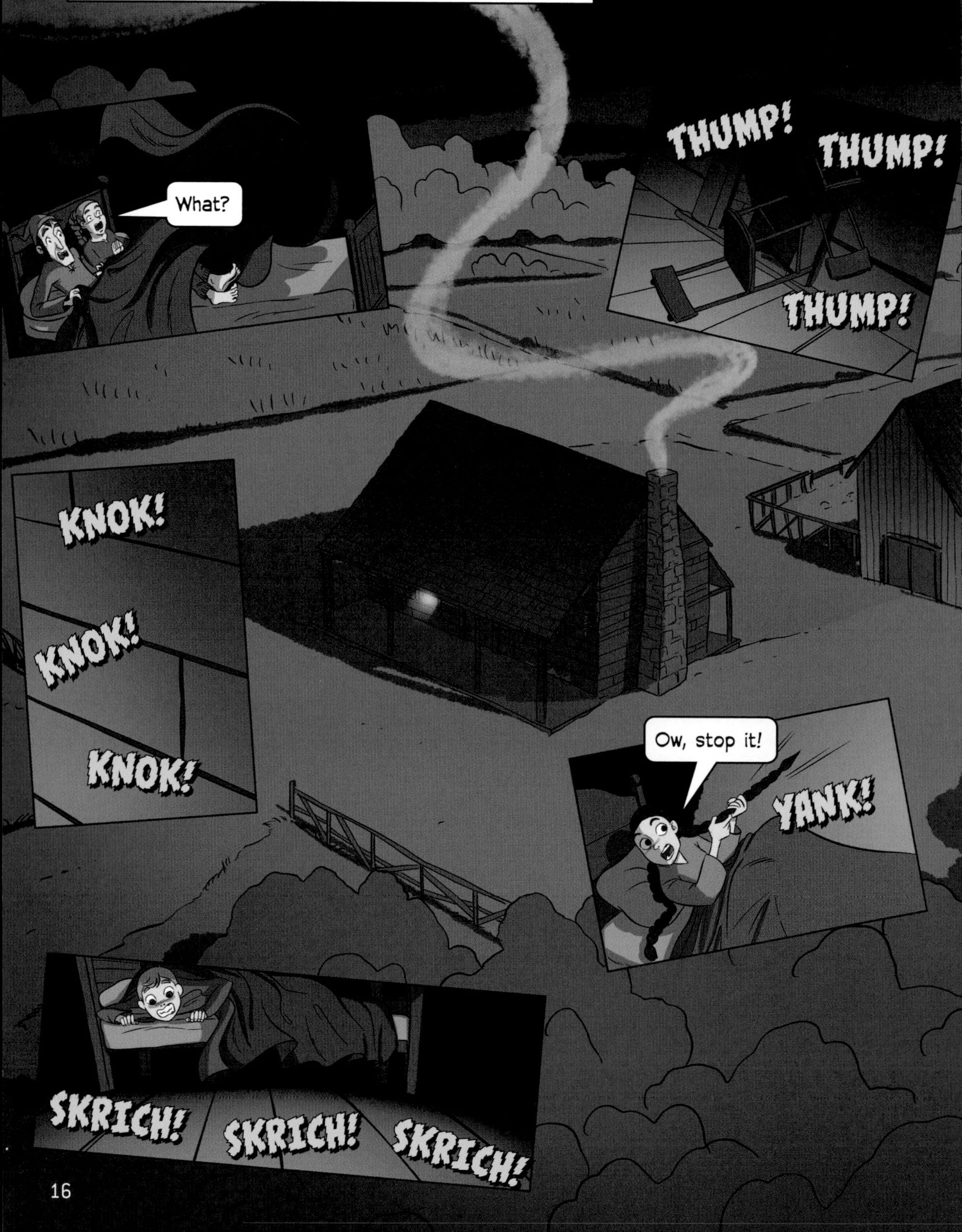

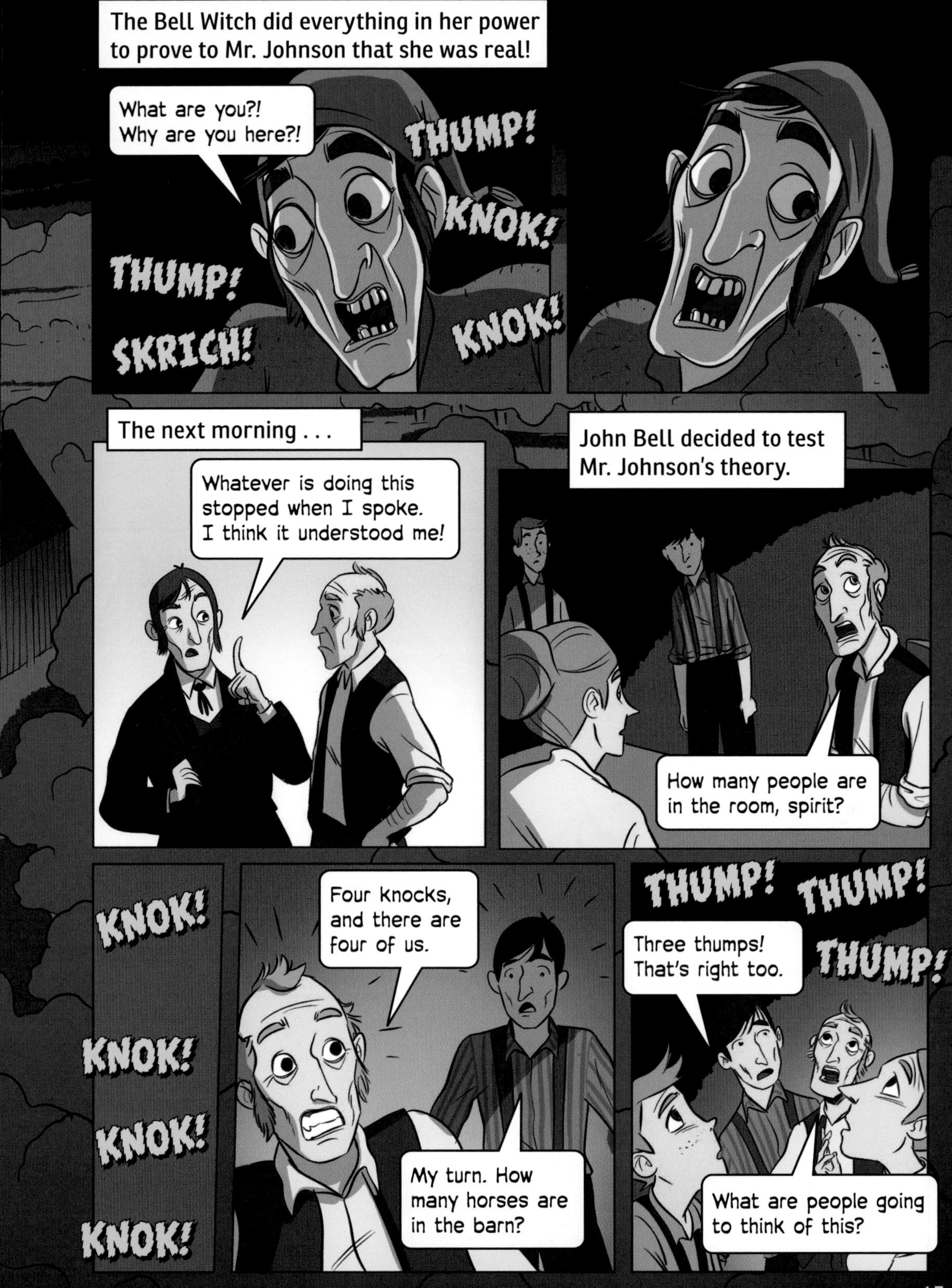

The Bell Witch did everything in her power to prove to Mr. Johnson that she was real!
What are you?! Why are you here?!
THUMP!
KNOK!
THUMP!
SKRICH!
KNOK!
The next morning . . .
Whatever is doing this stopped when I spoke. I think it understood me!
John Bell decided to test Mr. Johnson's theory.
How many people are in the room, spirit?
KNOK!
KNOK!
KNOK!
KNOK!
Four knocks, and there are four of us.
My turn. How many horses are in the barn?
THUMP!
THUMP!
Three thumps! That's right too.
THUMP!
What are people going to think of this?

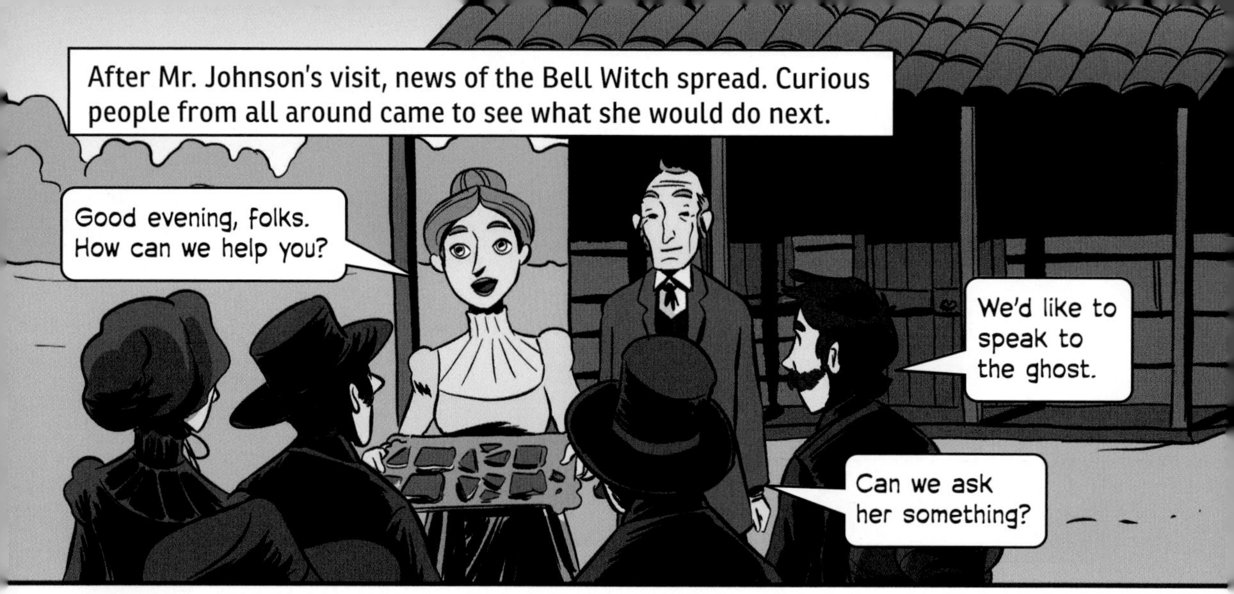
After Mr. Johnson's visit, news of the Bell Witch spread. Curious people from all around came to see what she would do next.
Good evening, folks. How can we help you?
We'd like to speak to the ghost.
Can we ask her something?

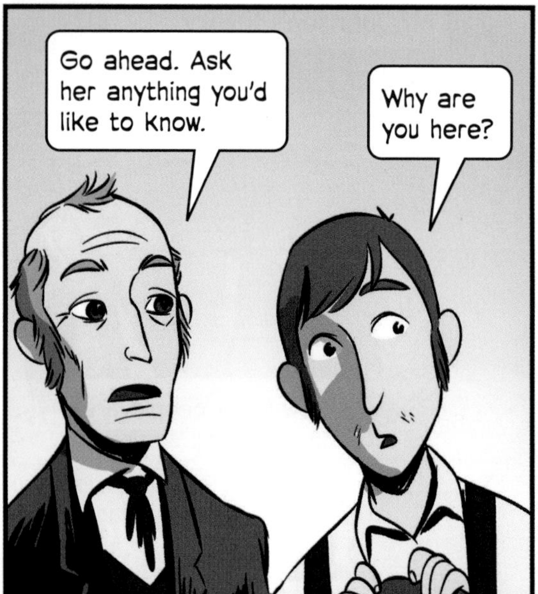
Go ahead. Ask her anything you'd like to know.
Why are you here?

At first, the ghost only answered in whistling noises.

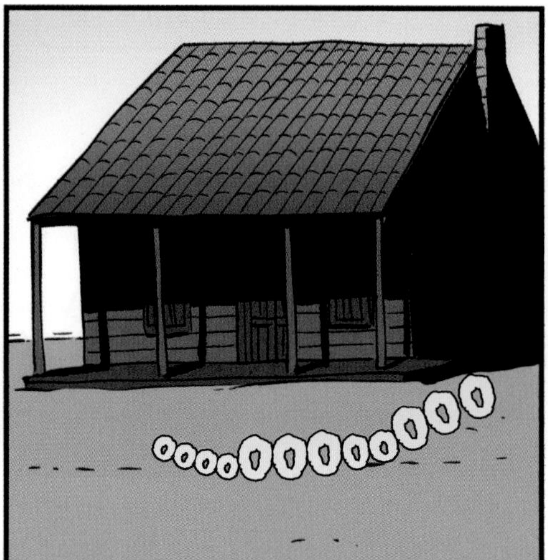

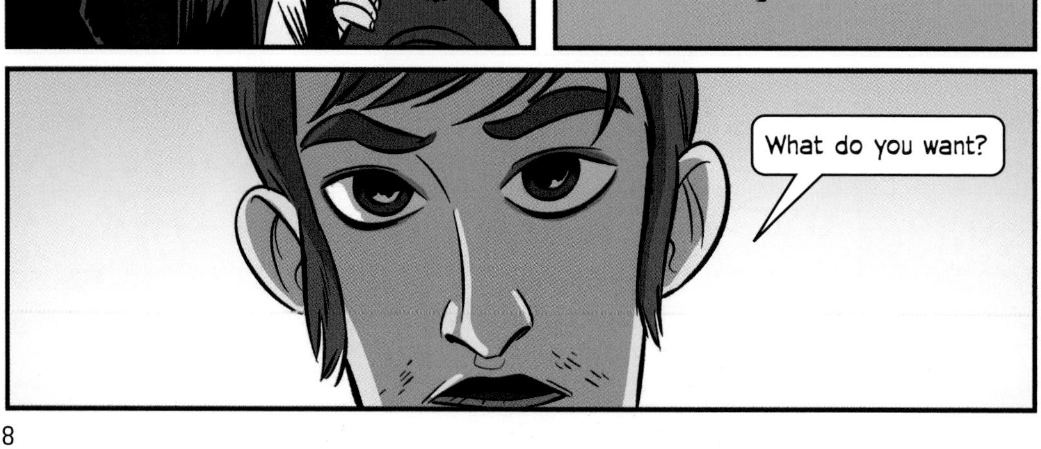
What do you want?

But then her voice grew into a whisper.

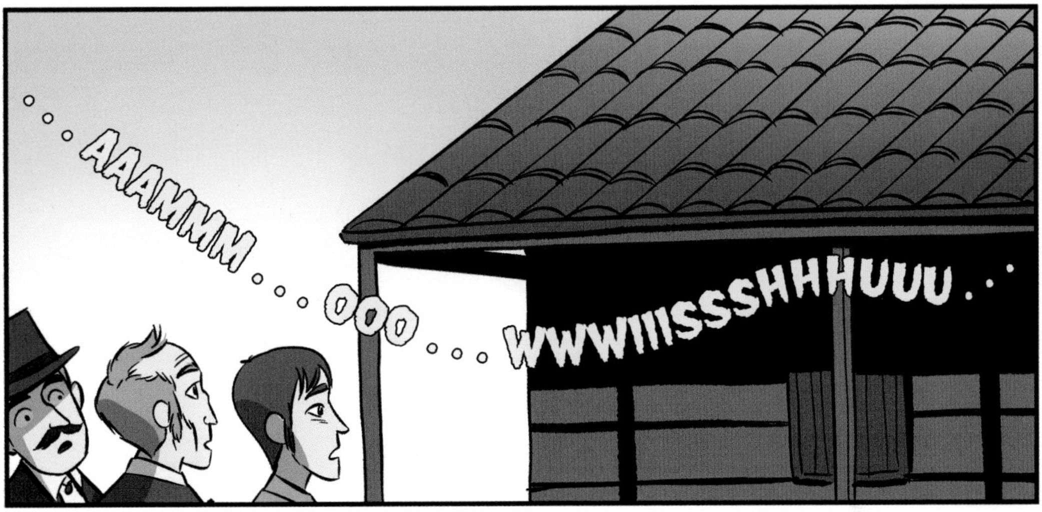

. . . AAAMMMM . . . OOO . . . WWWIIISSSHHHUUU . . .

Finally, she began to speak.

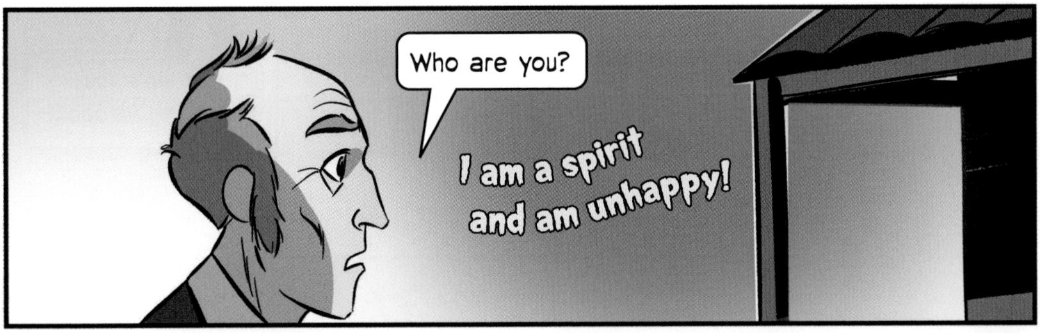

Who are you?
I am a spirit and am unhappy!

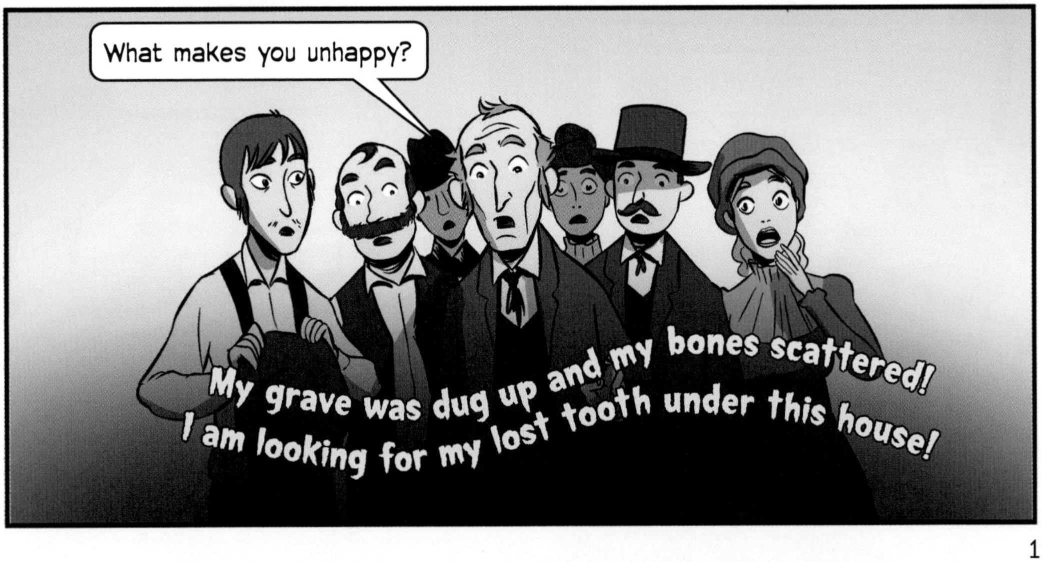

What makes you unhappy?
My grave was dug up and my bones scattered! I am looking for my lost tooth under this house!

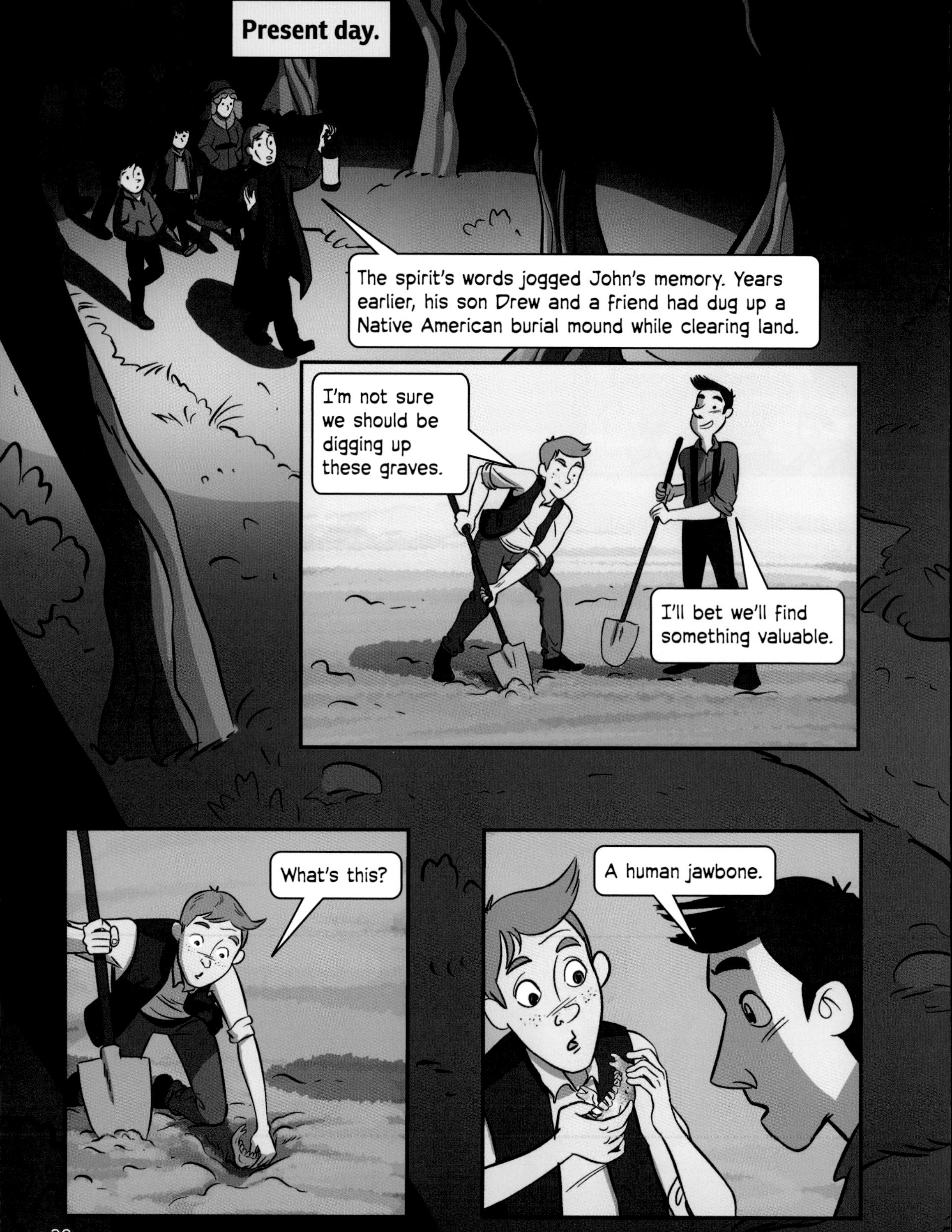
Present day.
The spirit's words jogged John's memory. Years earlier, his son Drew and a friend had dug up a Native American burial mound while clearing land.
I'm not sure we should be digging up these graves.
I'll bet we'll find something valuable.
What's this?
A human jawbone.

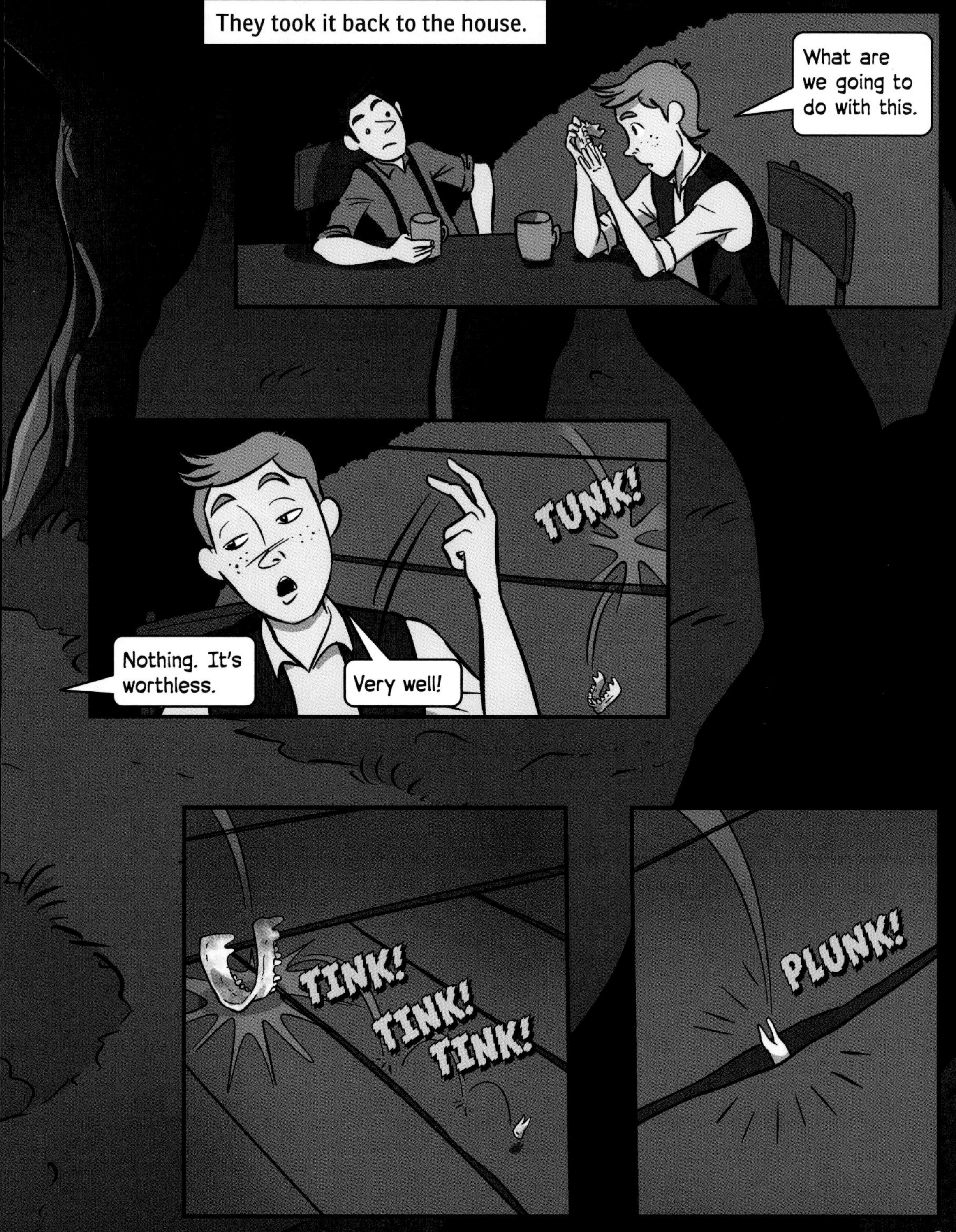
They took it back to the house.
What are we going to do with this.
Nothing. It's worthless.
Very well!
TUNK!
TINK!
TINK!
TINK!
PLUNK!

Fall, 1818. The Bell Farm. John questioned Drew.

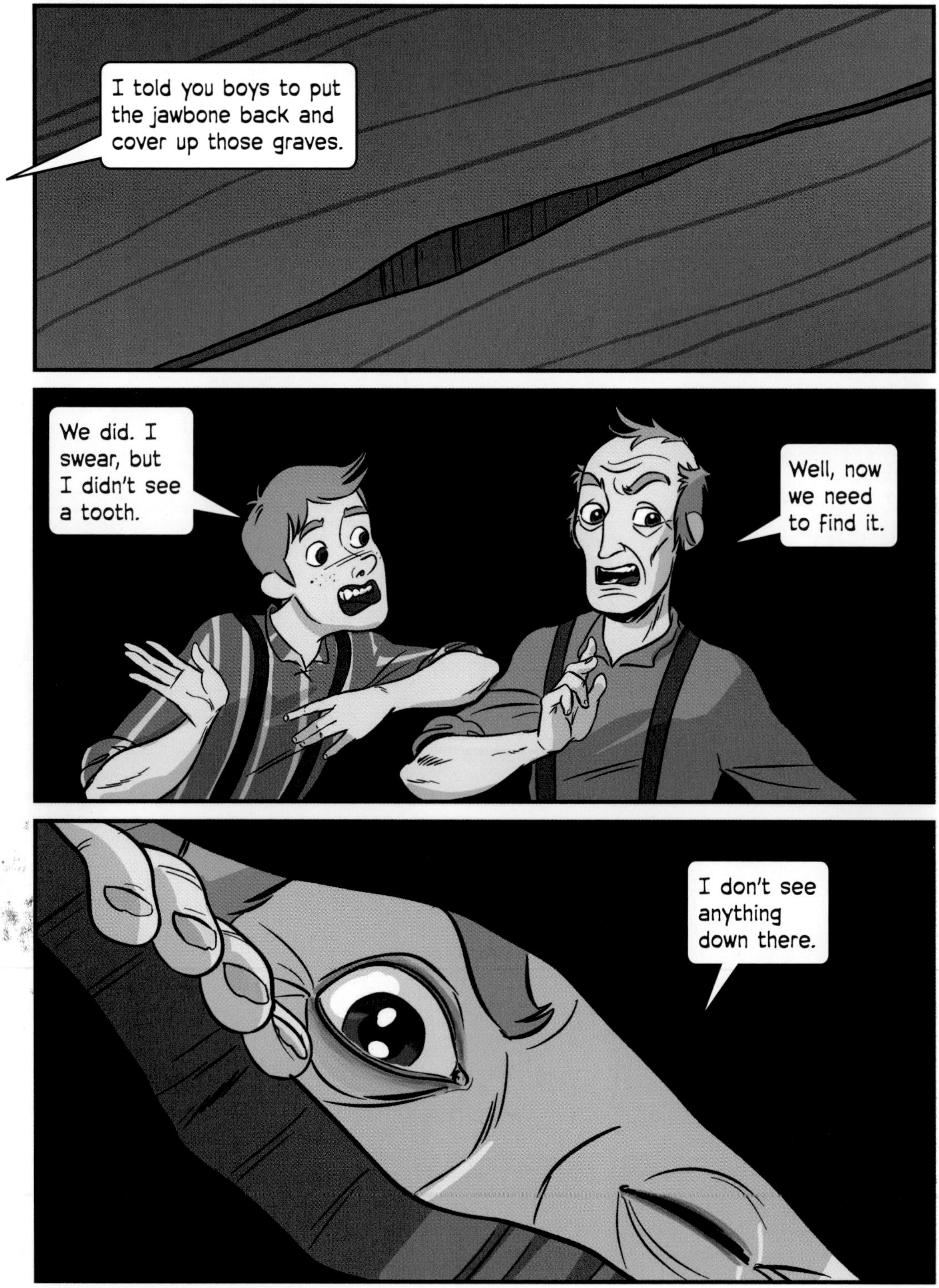
I told you boys to put the jawbone back and cover up those graves.
We did. I swear, but I didn't see a tooth.
Well, now we need to find it.
I don't see anything down there.

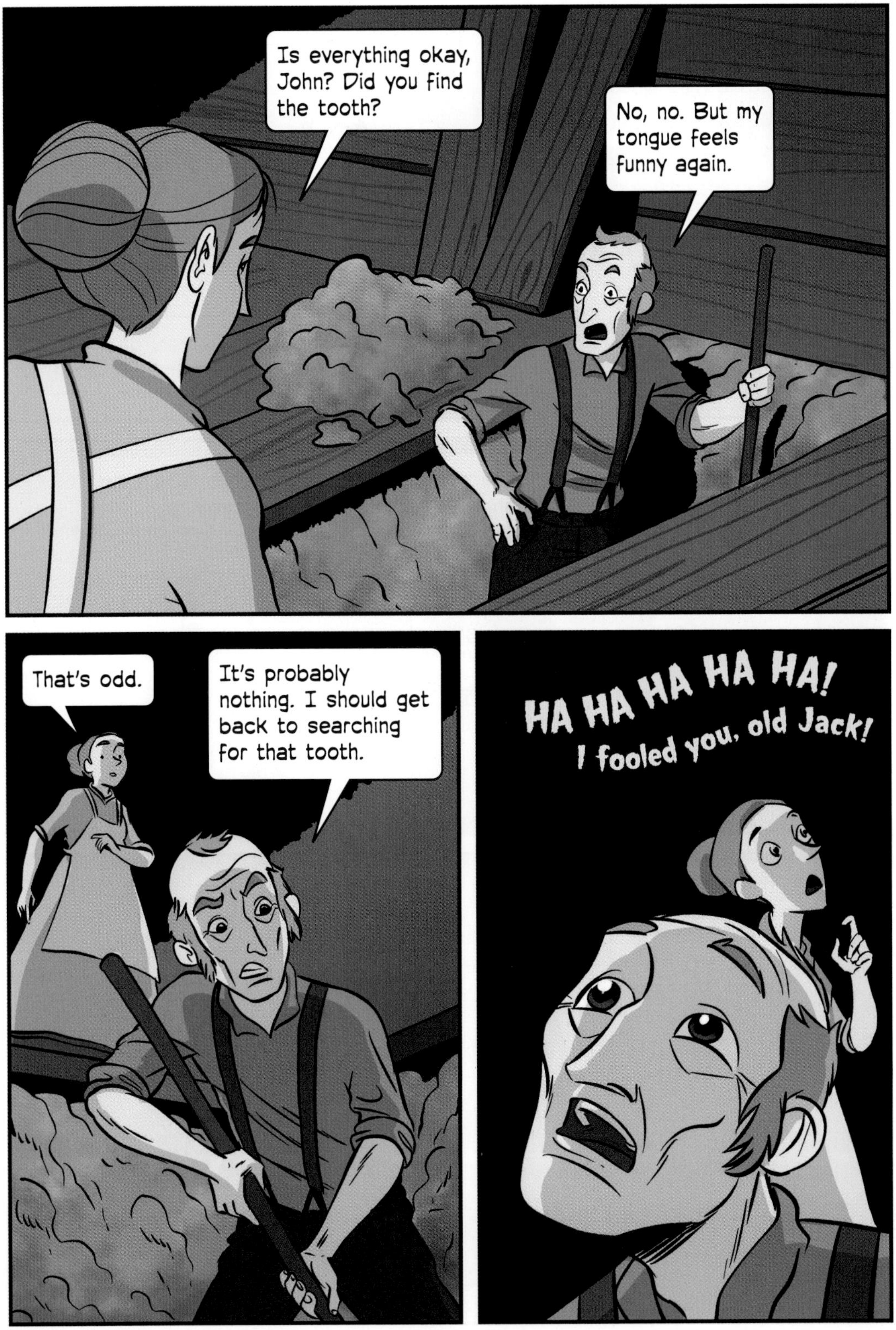
Is everything okay, John? Did you find the tooth?
No, no. But my tongue feels funny again.
That's odd.
It's probably nothing. I should get back to searching for that tooth.
HA HA HA HA HA!
I fooled you, old Jack!

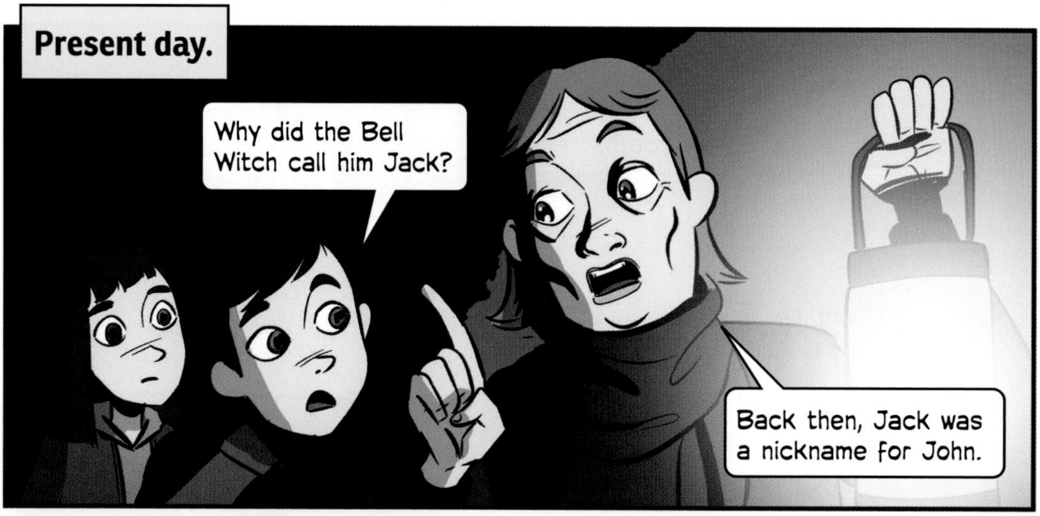
Present day.
Why did the Bell Witch call him Jack?
Back then, Jack was a nickname for John.

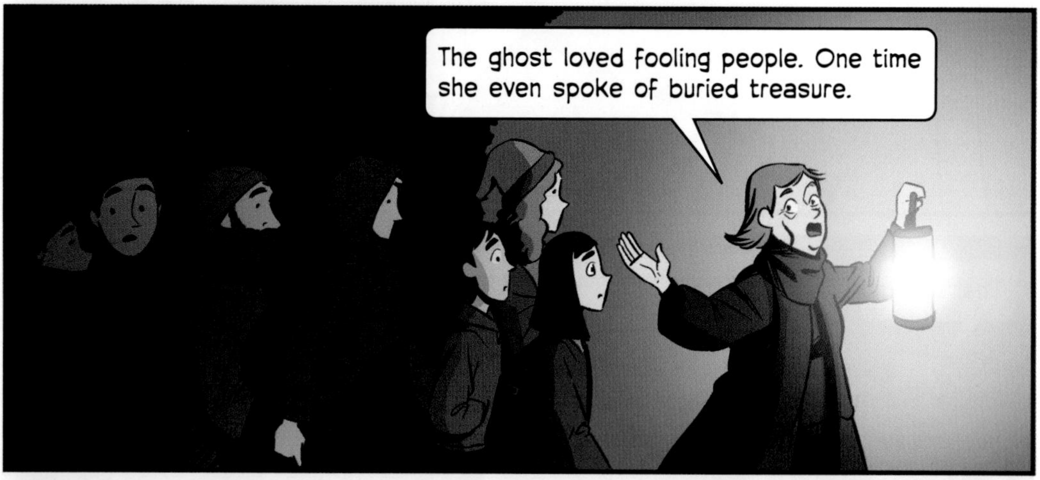
The ghost loved fooling people. One time she even spoke of buried treasure.

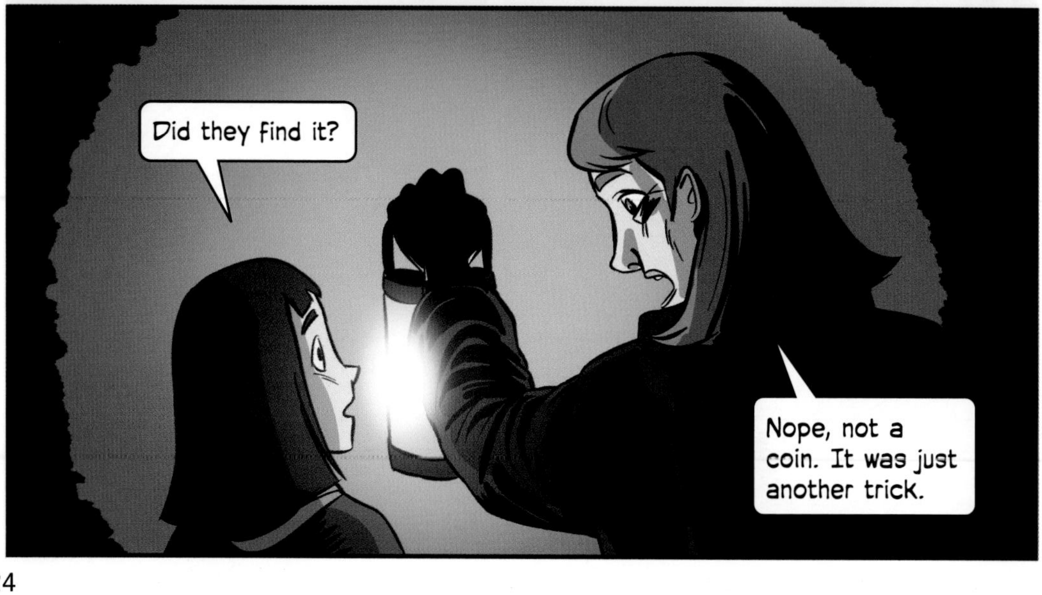
Did they find it?
Nope, not a coin. It was just another trick.

Then one day a local reverend asked the Bell Witch a question.

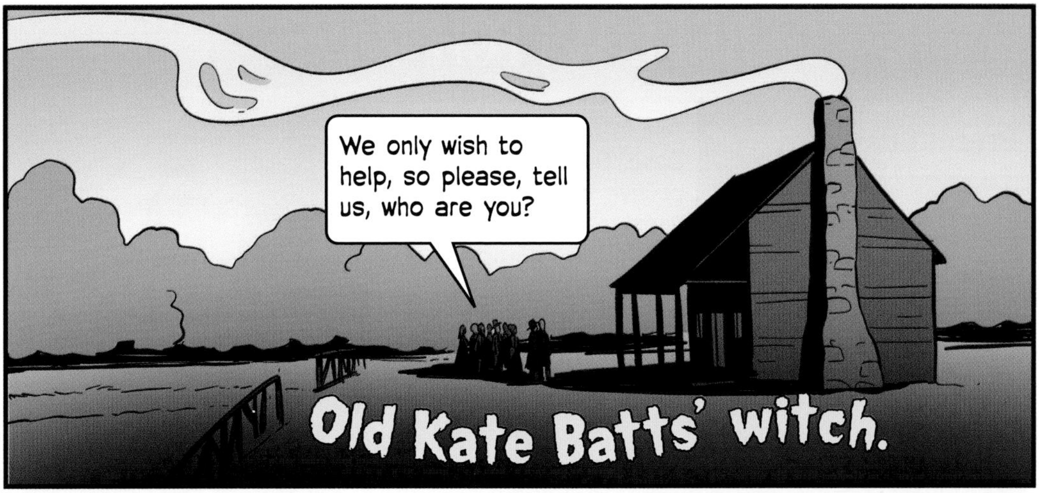

We only wish to help, so please, tell us, who are you?
Old Kate Batts' witch.

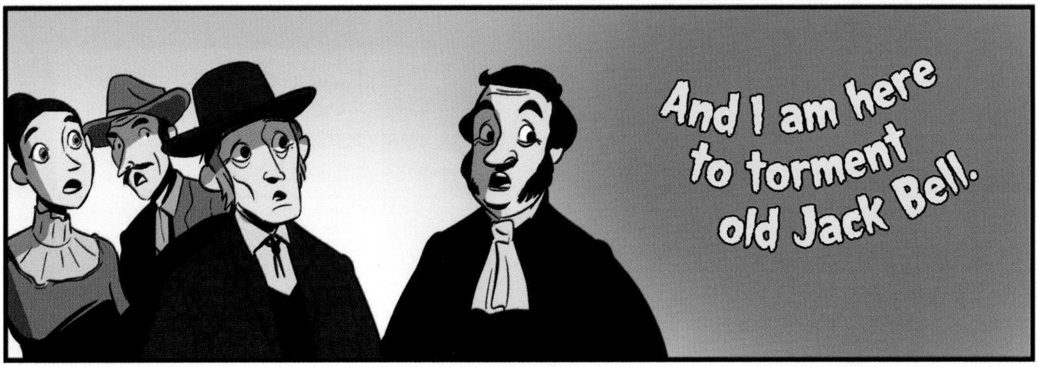

And I am here to torment old Jack Bell.

Kate Batts was a local woman who some people believed was a witch.

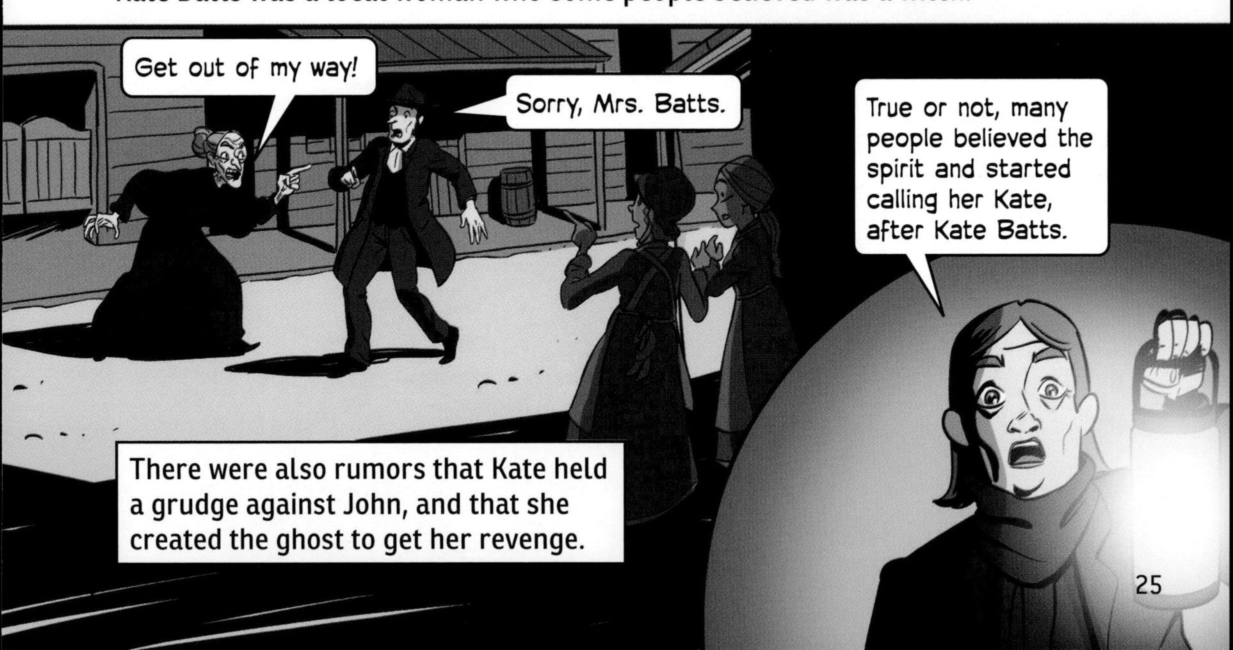

Get out of my way!
Sorry, Mrs. Batts.
True or not, many people believed the spirit and started calling her Kate, after Kate Batts.
There were also rumors that Kate held a grudge against John, and that she created the ghost to get her revenge.

CHAPTER 3

BELL WITCH CAVE

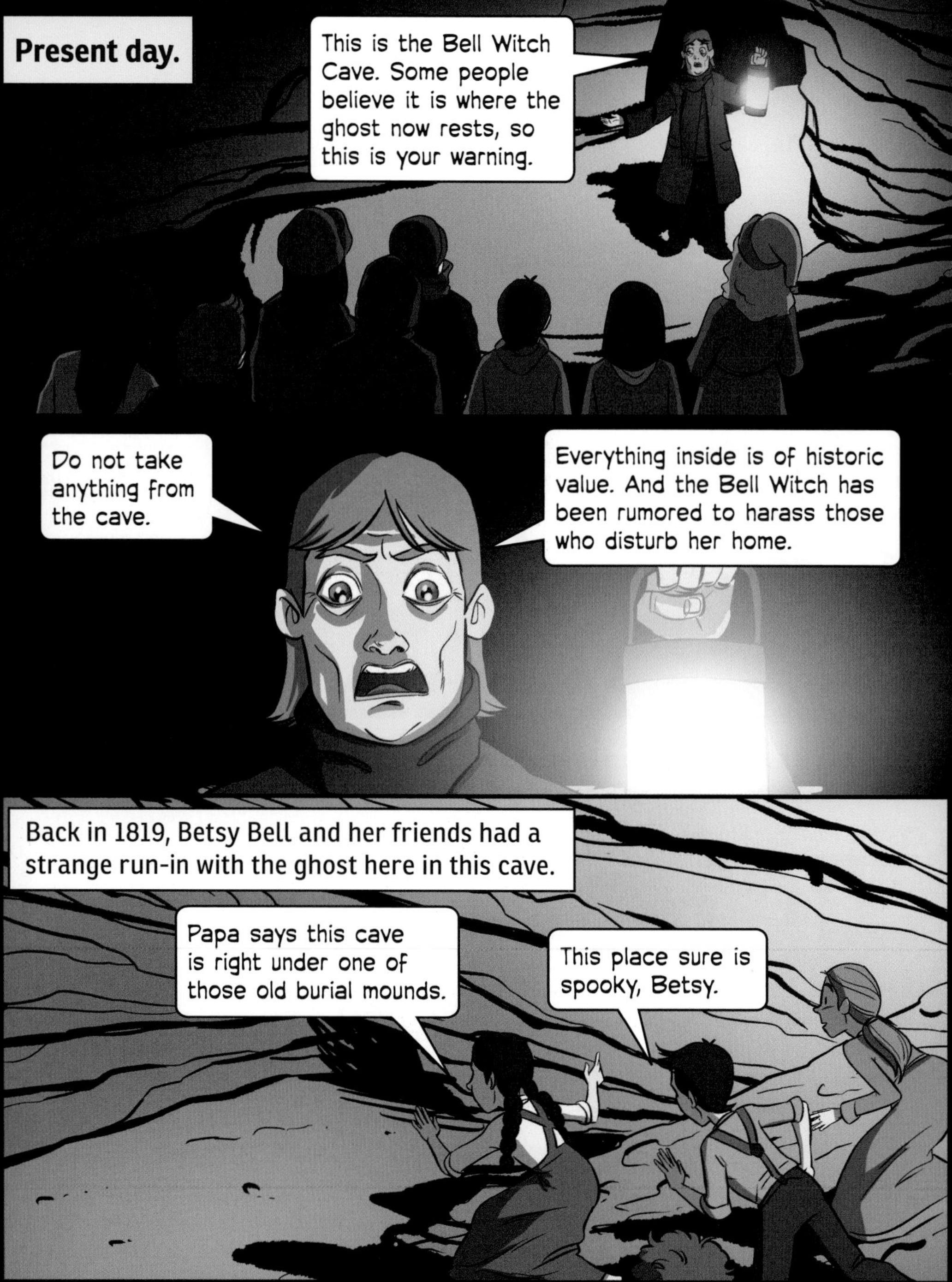
Present day.
This is the Bell Witch Cave. Some people believe it is where the ghost now rests, so this is your warning.
Do not take anything from the cave.
Everything inside is of historic value. And the Bell Witch has been rumored to harass those who disturb her home.
Back in 1819, Betsy Bell and her friends had a strange run-in with the ghost here in this cave.
Papa says this cave is right under one of those old burial mounds.
This place sure is spooky, Betsy.

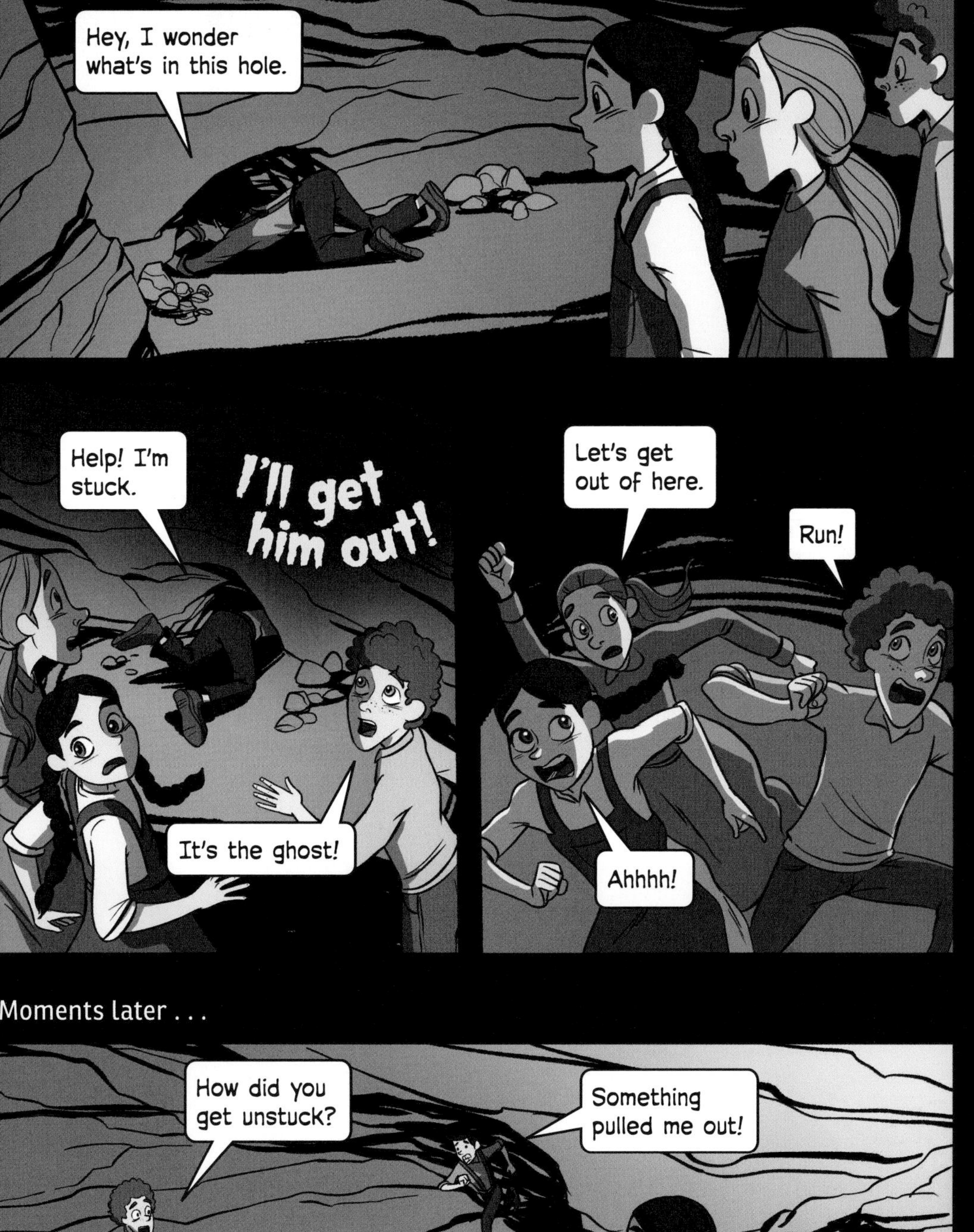
Hey, I wonder what's in this hole.
Help! I'm stuck.
I'll get him out!
It's the ghost!
Let's get out of here.
Run!
Ahhhh!

Moments later . . .

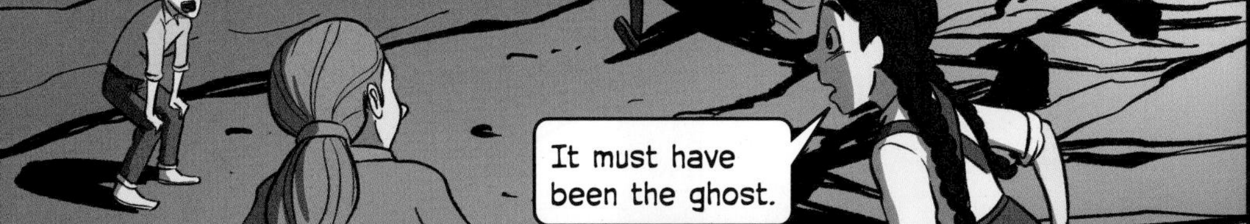
How did you get unstuck?
Something pulled me out!
It must have been the ghost.

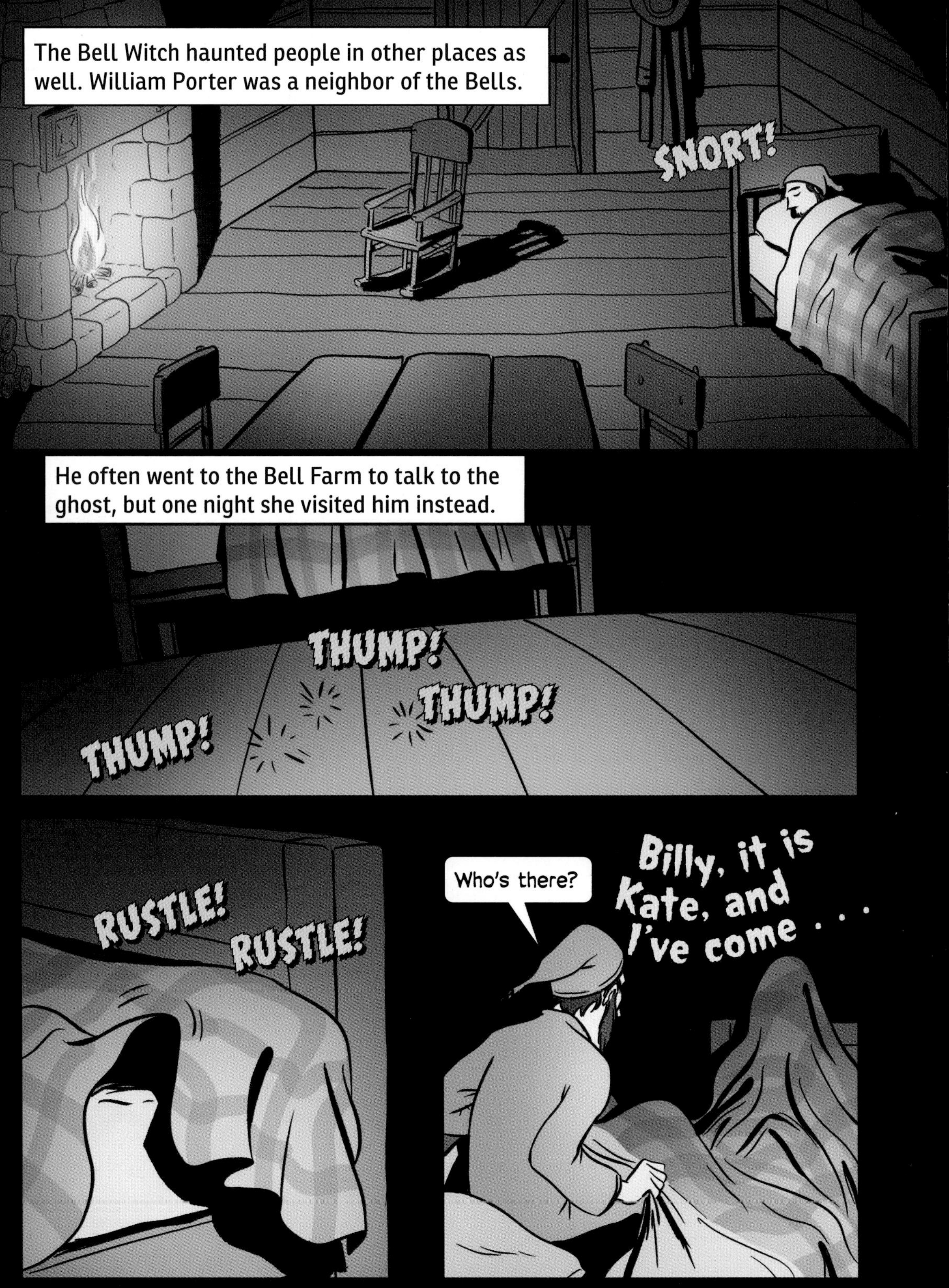
The Bell Witch haunted people in other places as well. William Porter was a neighbor of the Bells.
SNORT!
He often went to the Bell Farm to talk to the ghost, but one night she visited him instead.
THUMP!
THUMP!
THUMP!
RUSTLE!
RUSTLE!
Who's there?
Billy, it is Kate, and I've come . . .

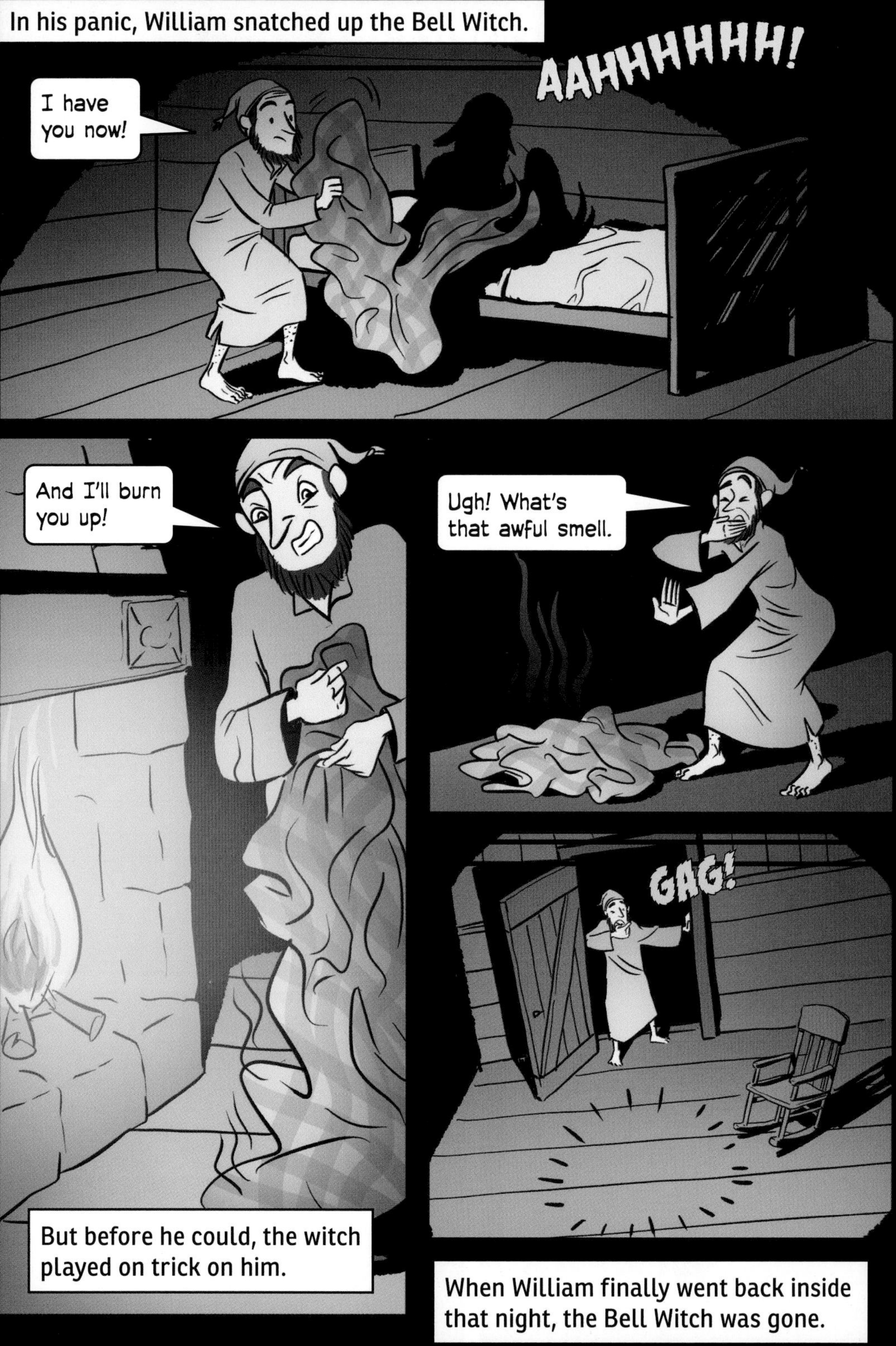
In his panic, William snatched up the Bell Witch.
I have you now!
AAHHHHHH!
And I'll burn you up!
But before he could, the witch played on trick on him.
Ugh! What's that awful smell.
GAG!
When William finally went back inside that night, the Bell Witch was gone.

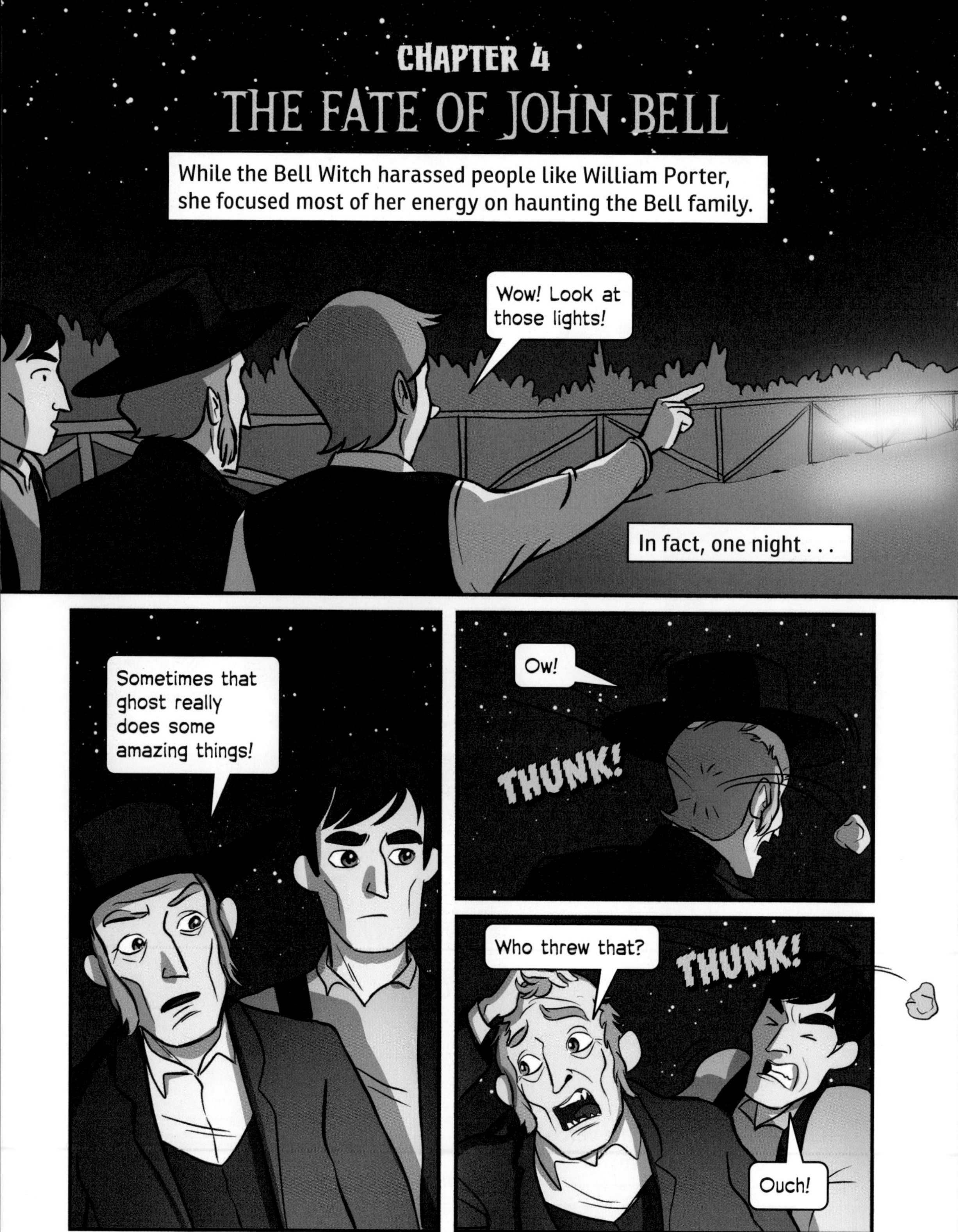
CHAPTER 4
THE FATE OF JOHN BELL
While the Bell Witch harassed people like William Porter, she focused most of her energy on haunting the Bell family.
Wow! Look at those lights!
In fact, one night . . .
Sometimes that ghost really does some amazing things!
Ow!
THUNK!
Who threw that?
THUNK!
Ouch!

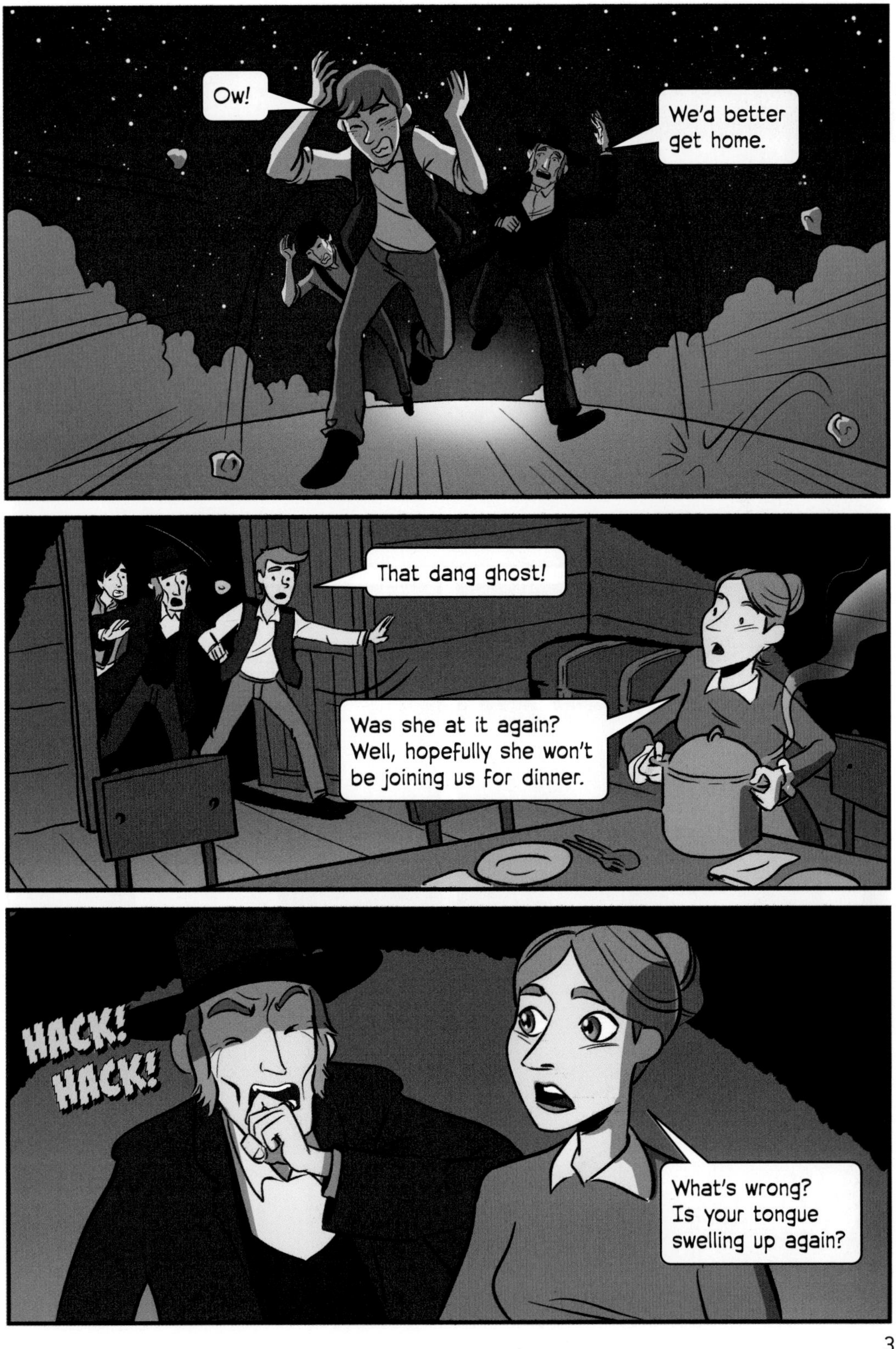
Ow!
We'd better get home.
That dang ghost!
Was she at it again? Well, hopefully she won't be joining us for dinner.
HACK! HACK!
What's wrong? Is your tongue swelling up again?

And the ghost often tormented young Betsy.

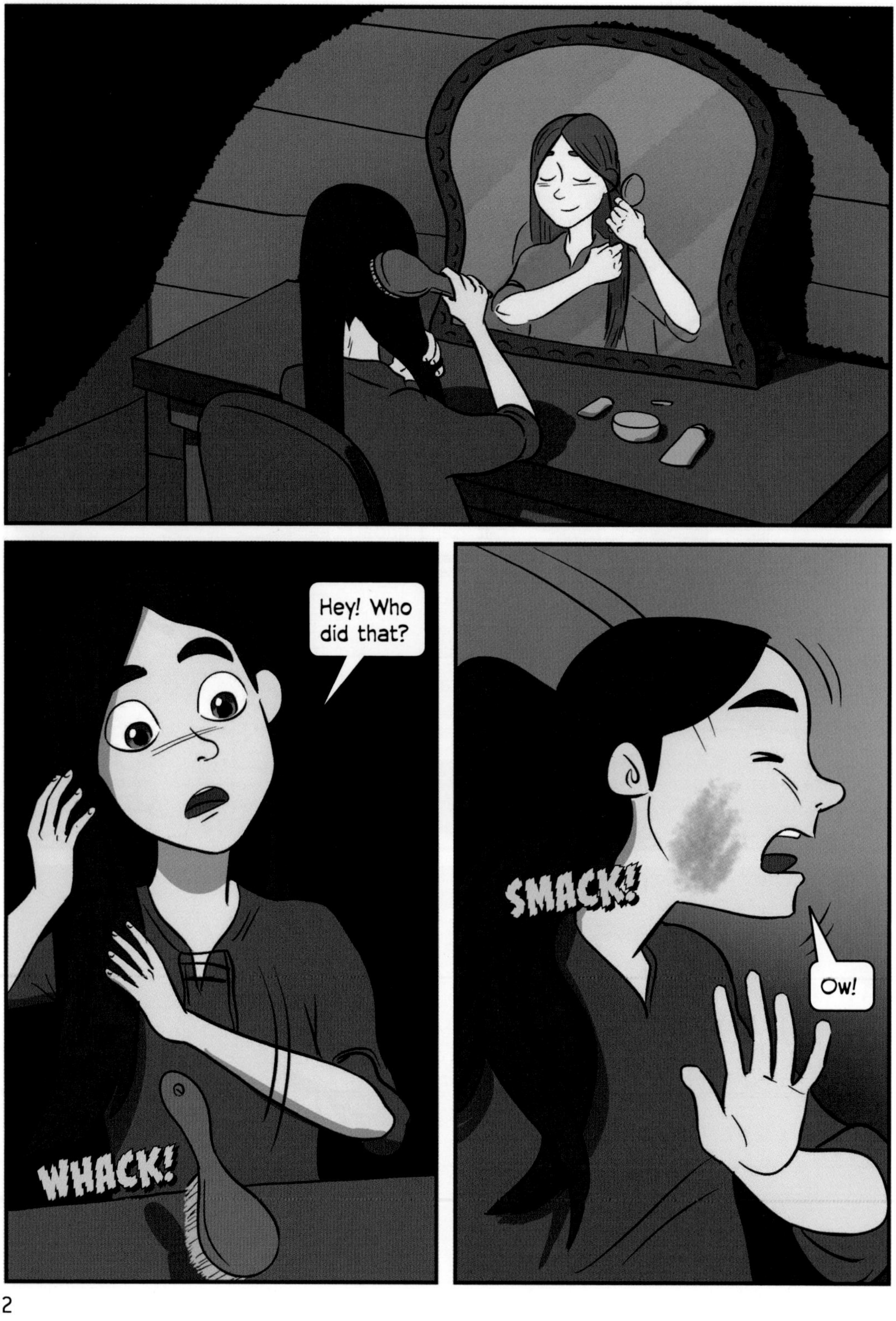
Hey! Who did that?
WHACK!
SMACK!
Ow!

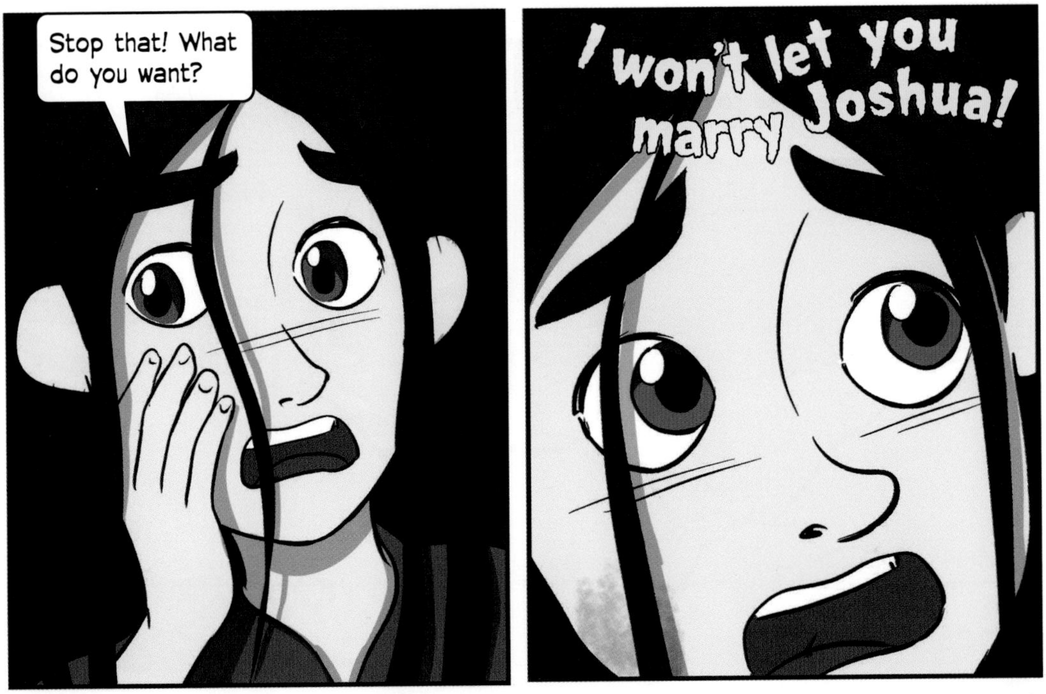
Stop that! What do you want?
I won't let you marry Joshua!

As the hauntings continued, the ghost punished Betsy for her plans to marry a young man from the area.

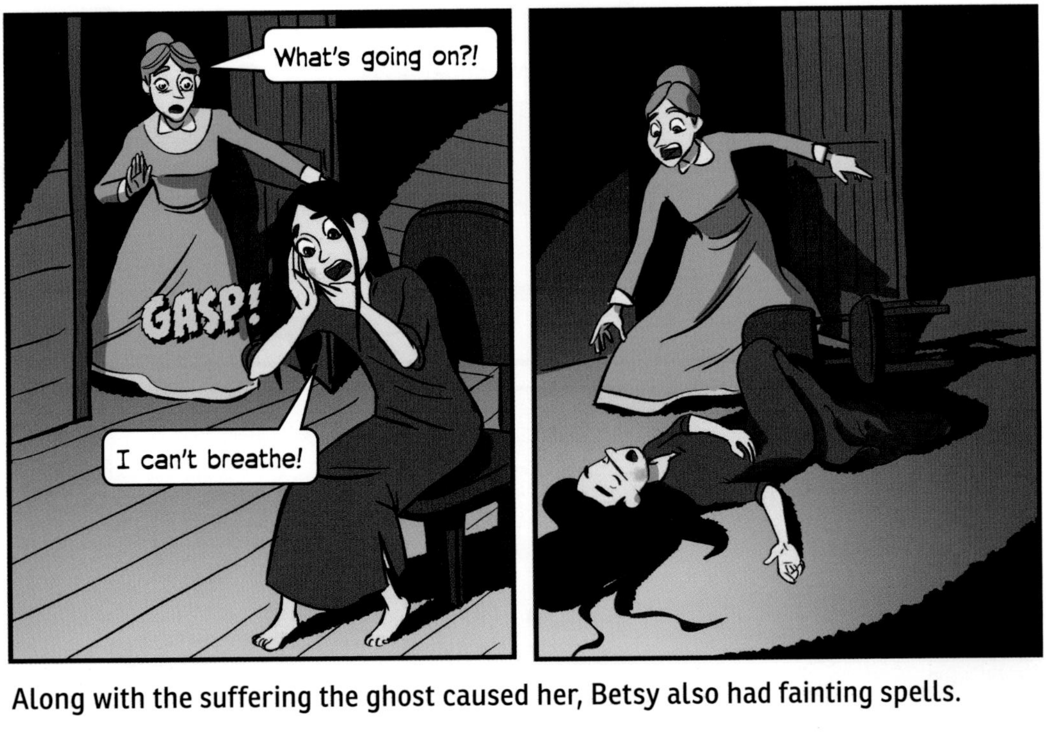
What's going on?!
GASP!
I can't breathe!

Along with the suffering the ghost caused her, Betsy also had fainting spells.

While the ghost pestered Betsy, no one suffered more than John Bell.

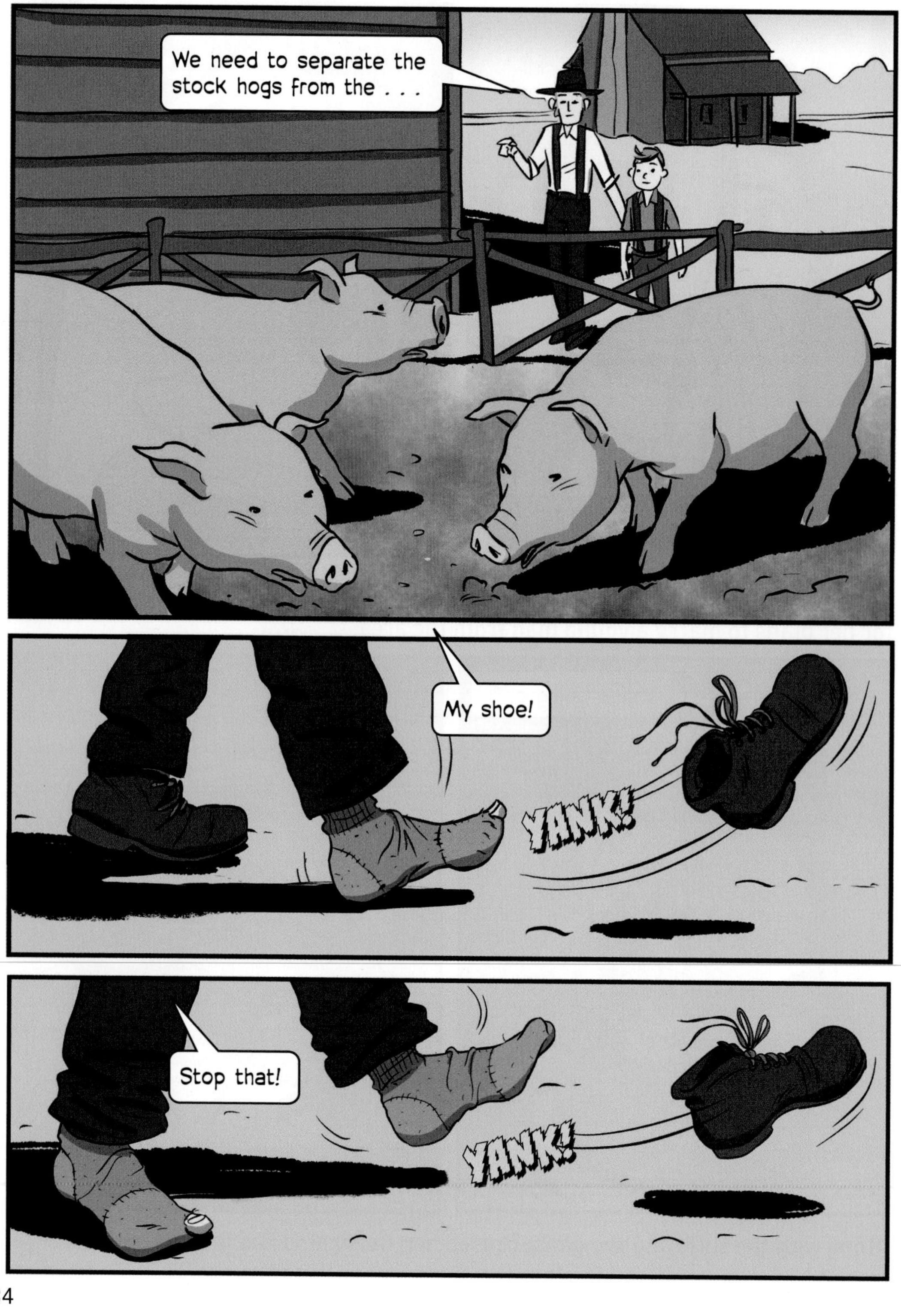
We need to separate the stock hogs from the . . .
My shoe!
YANK!
Stop that!
YANK!

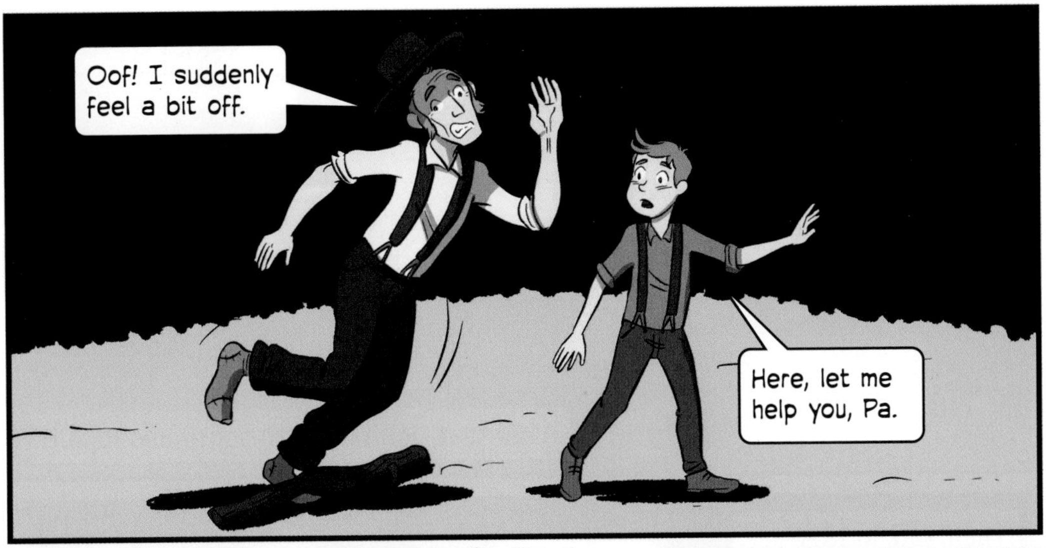
Oof! I suddenly feel a bit off.
Here, let me help you, Pa.

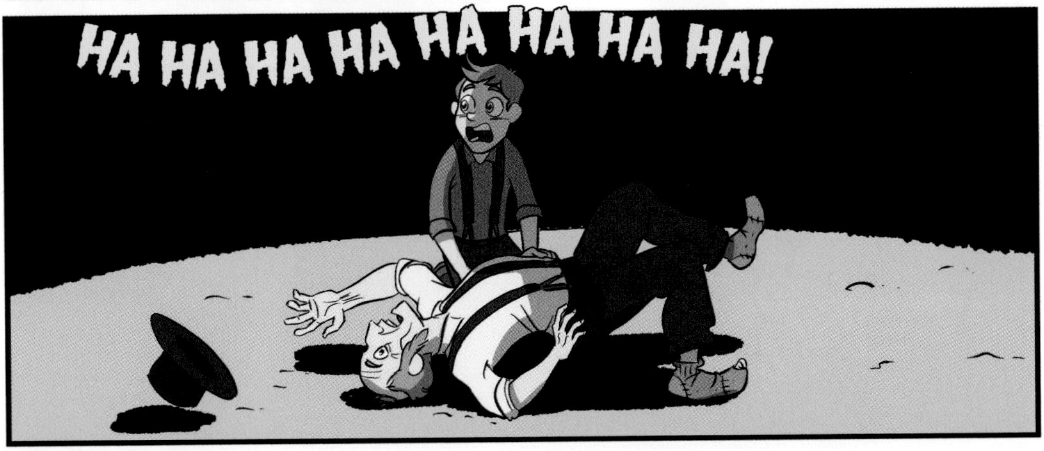
HA HA HA HA HA HA HA HA!

Since early on, John had been feeling a strange illness affecting him.

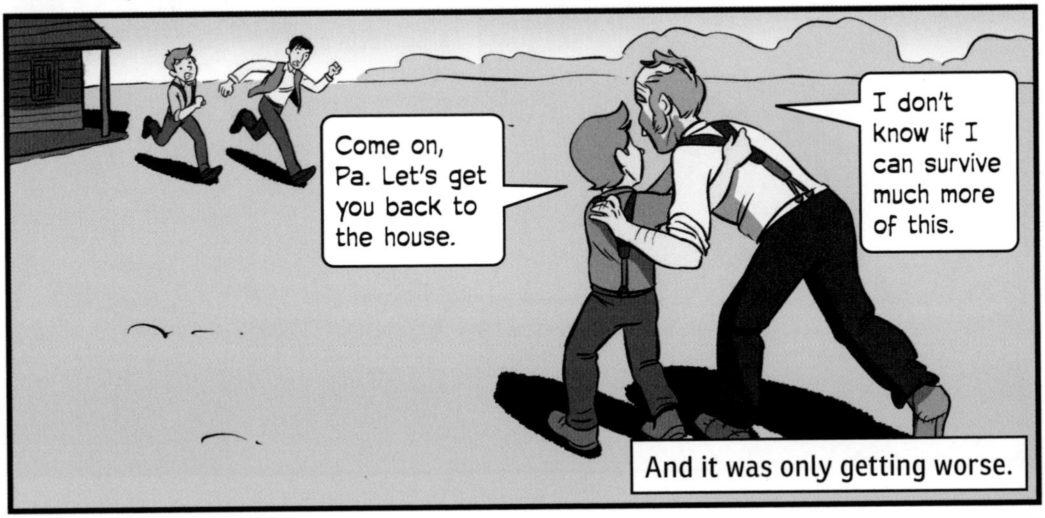
I don't know if I can survive much more of this.
Come on, Pa. Let's get you back to the house.
And it was only getting worse.

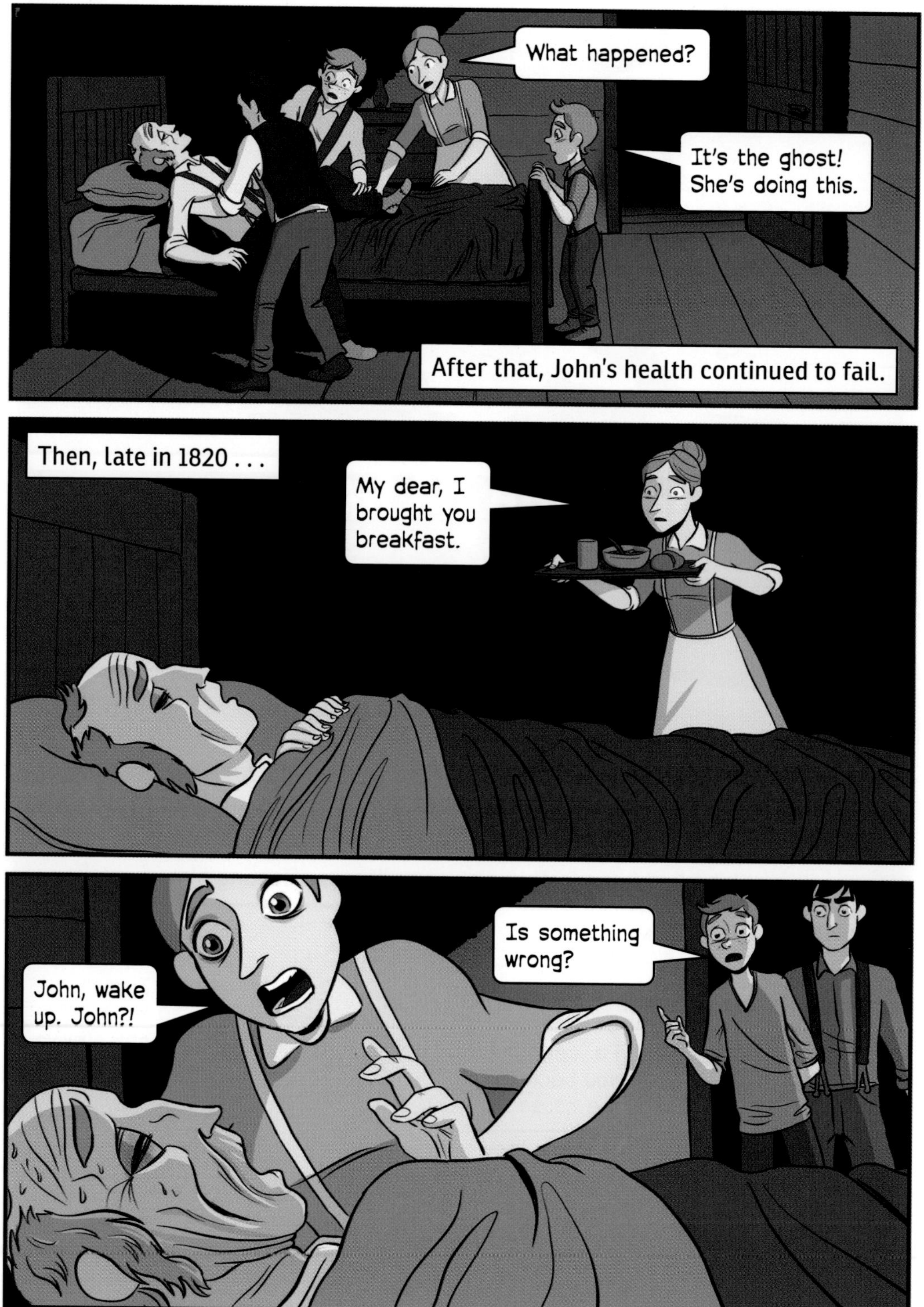
What happened?
It's the ghost! She's doing this.
After that, John's health continued to fail.
Then, late in 1820 . . .
My dear, I brought you breakfast.
Is something wrong?
John, wake up. John?!

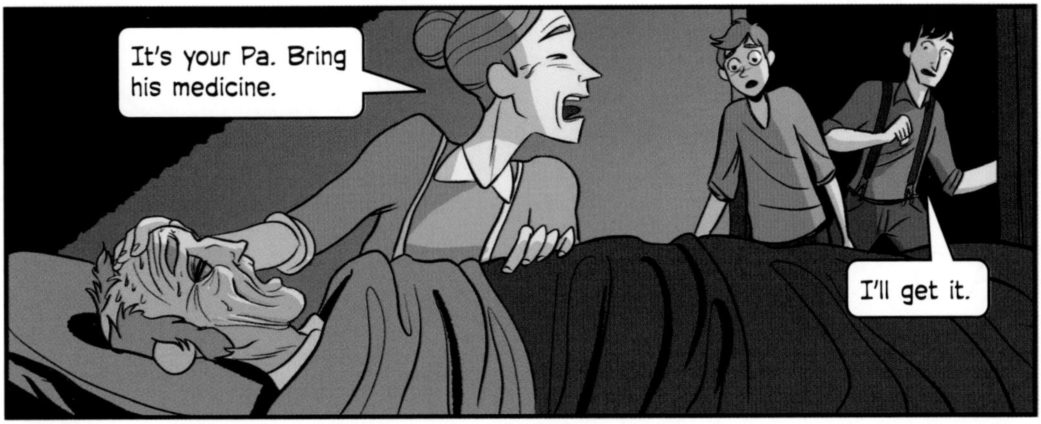
It's your Pa. Bring his medicine.
I'll get it.

Little did they know, the ghost was about to play one last trick on John Bell.

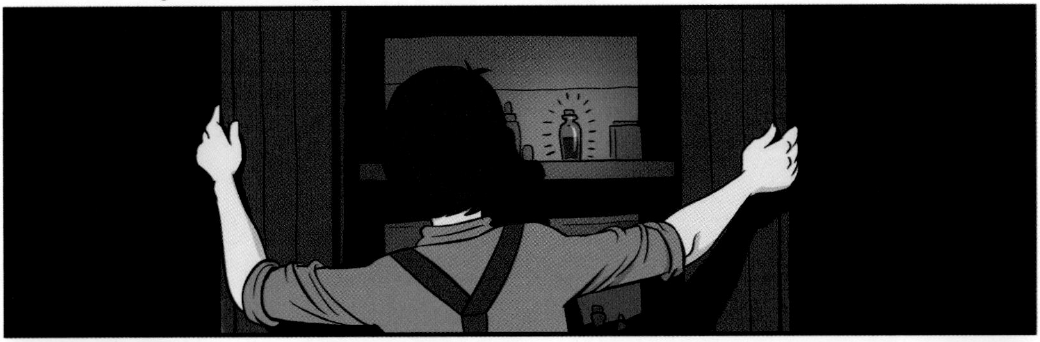

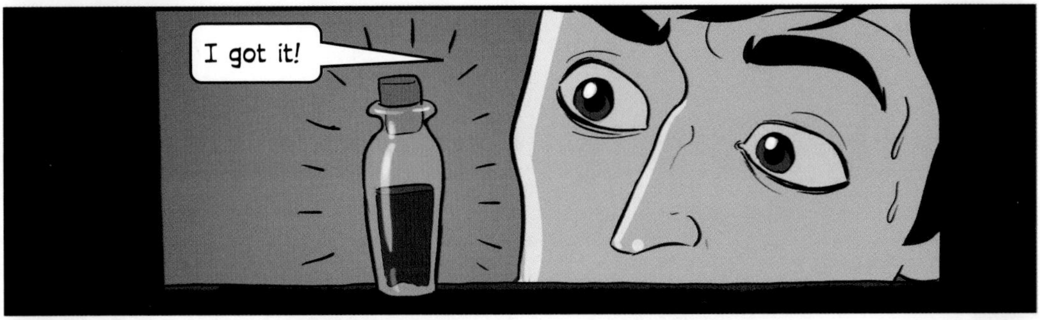
I got it!

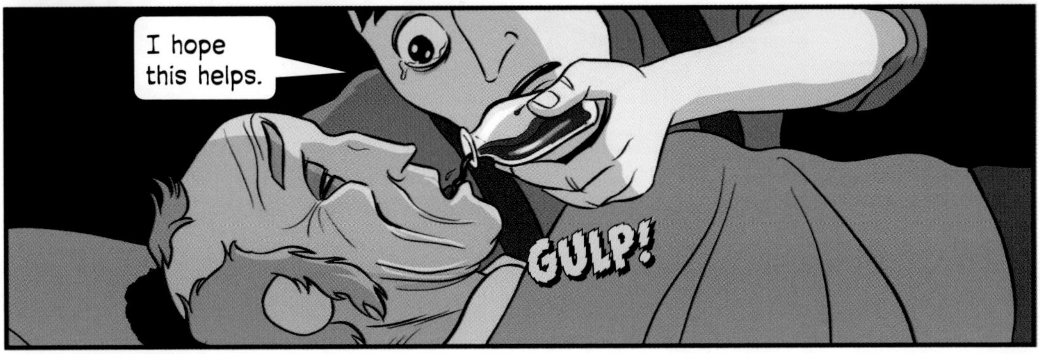
I hope this helps.
GULP!

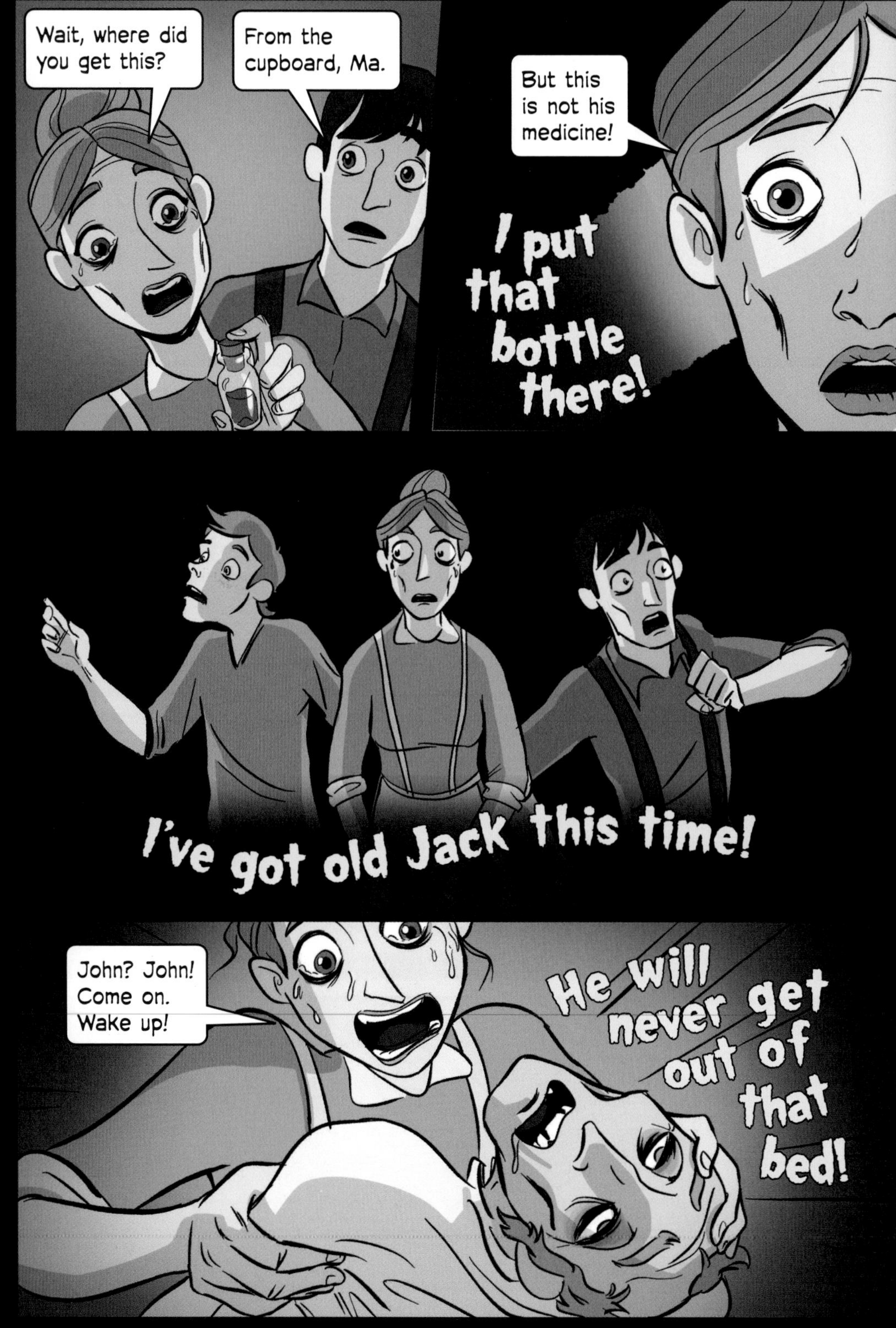
Wait, where did you get this?
From the cupboard, Ma.
But this is not his medicine!
I put that bottle there!
I've got old Jack this time!
John? John! Come on. Wake up!
He will never get out of that bed!

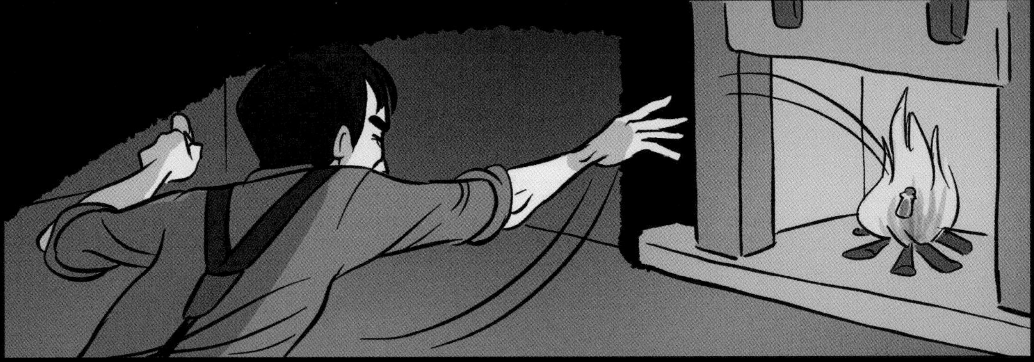

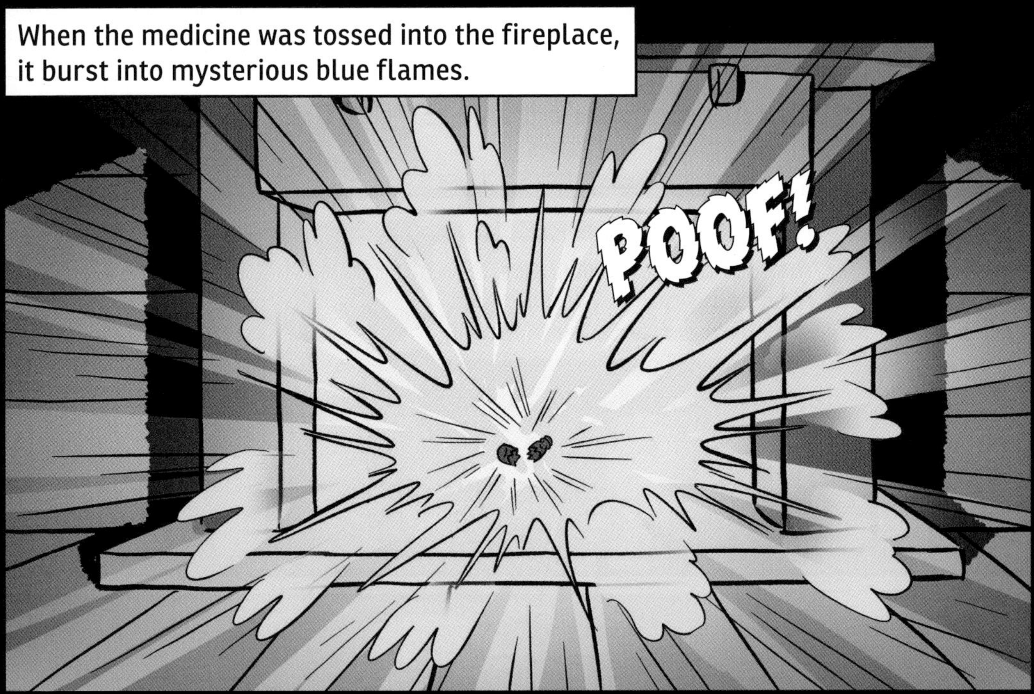
When the medicine was tossed into the fireplace, it burst into mysterious blue flames.
POOF!

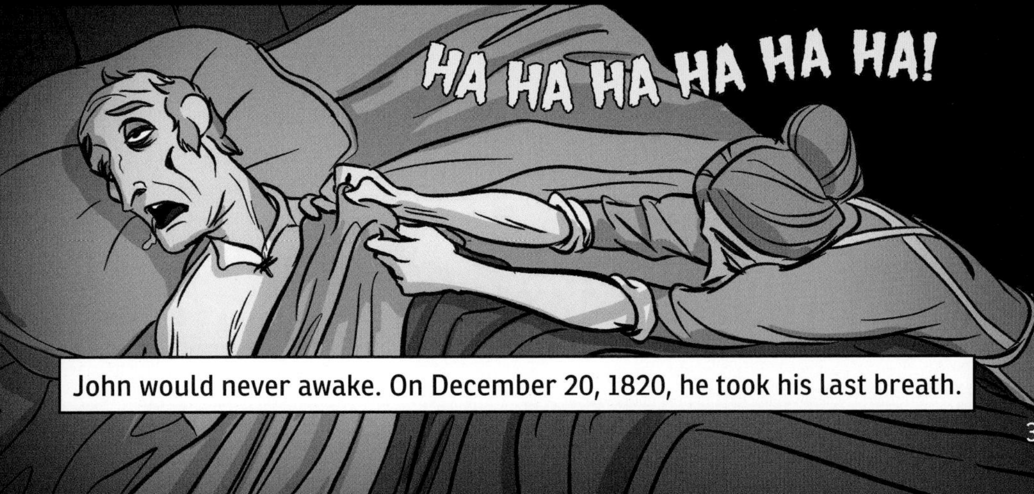
HA HA HA HA HA HA!
John would never awake. On December 20, 1820, he took his last breath.

CHAPTER 5
THE BELL WITCH'S RETURNS

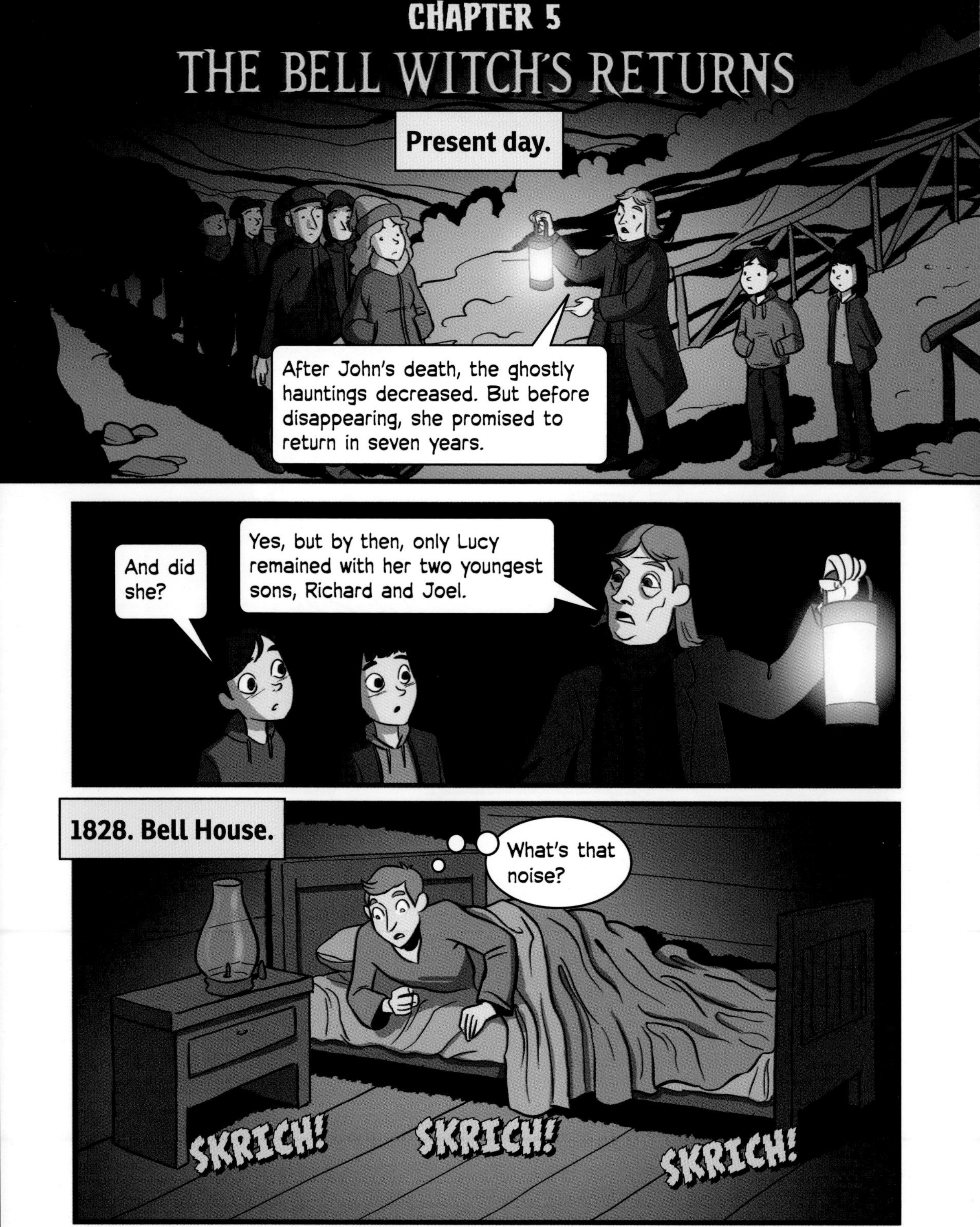

Present day.
After John's death, the ghostly hauntings decreased. But before disappearing, she promised to return in seven years.
And did she?
Yes, but by then, only Lucy remained with her two youngest sons, Richard and Joel.
1828. Bell House.
What's that noise?
SKRICH!
SKRICH!
SKRICH!

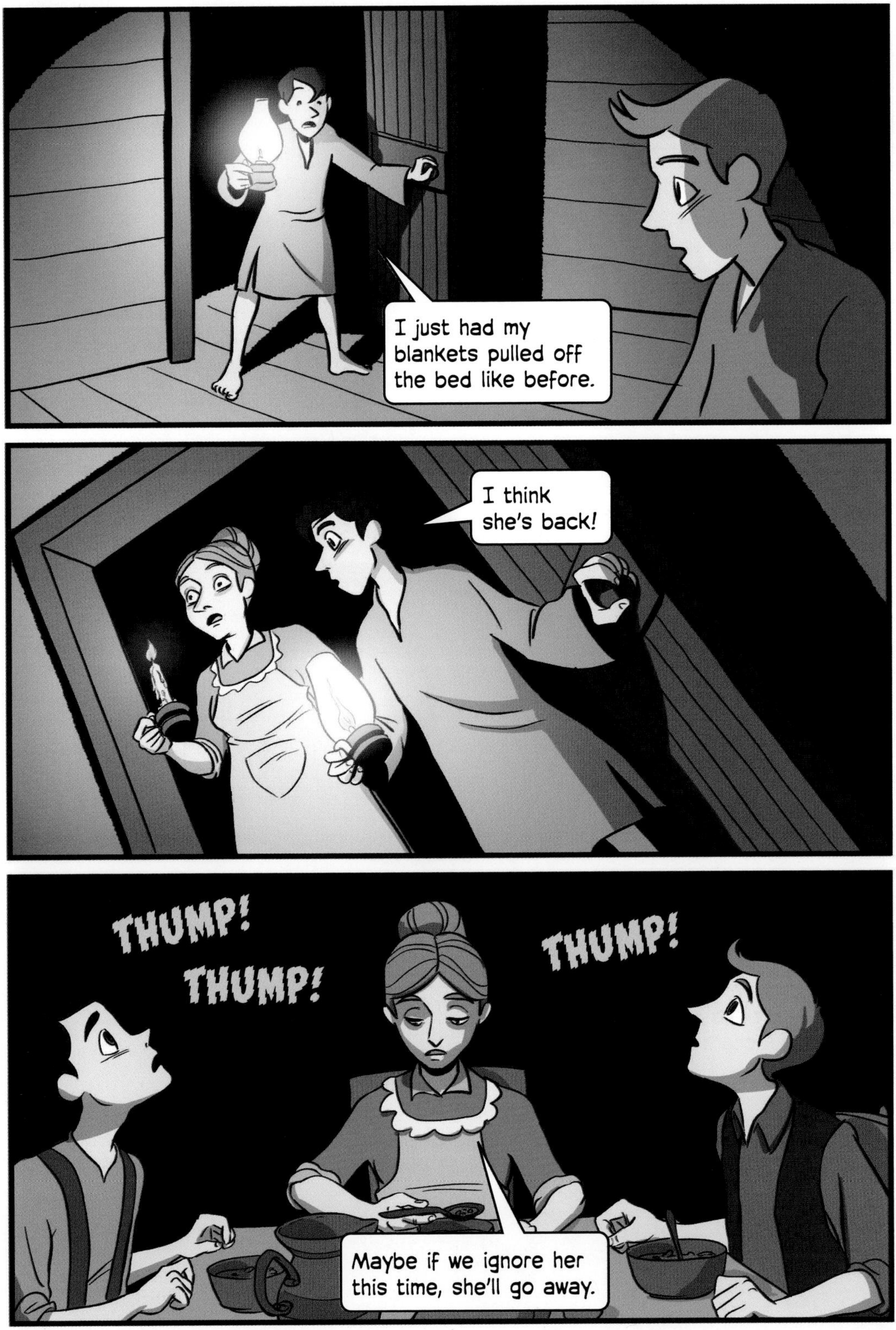
I just had my blankets pulled off the bed like before.
I think she's back!
THUMP!
THUMP!
THUMP!
Maybe if we ignore her this time, she'll go away.

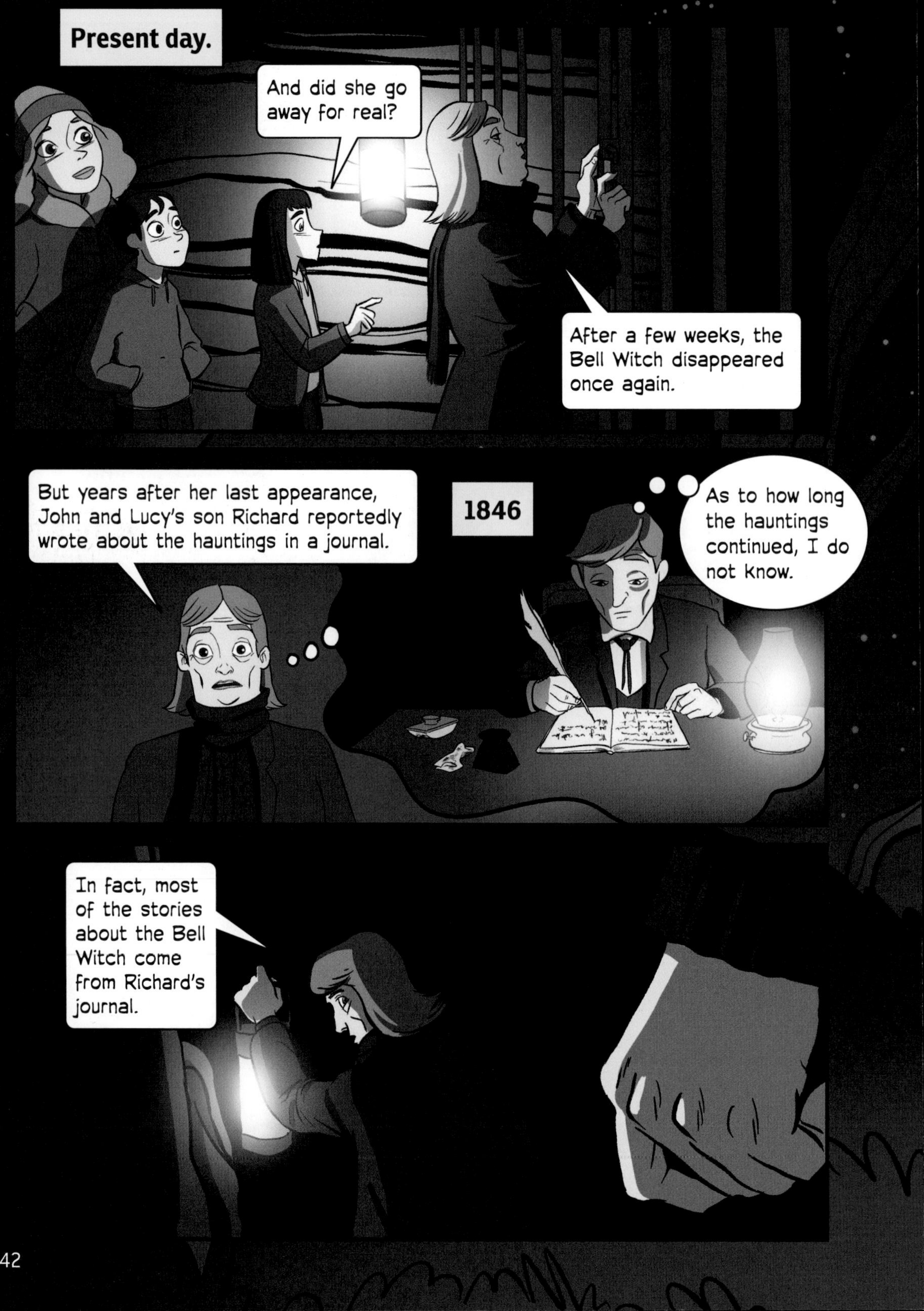
Present day.
And did she go away for real?
After a few weeks, the Bell Witch disappeared once again.
But years after her last appearance, John and Lucy's son Richard reportedly wrote about the hauntings in a journal.
1846
As to how long the hauntings continued, I do not know.
In fact, most of the stories about the Bell Witch come from Richard's journal.

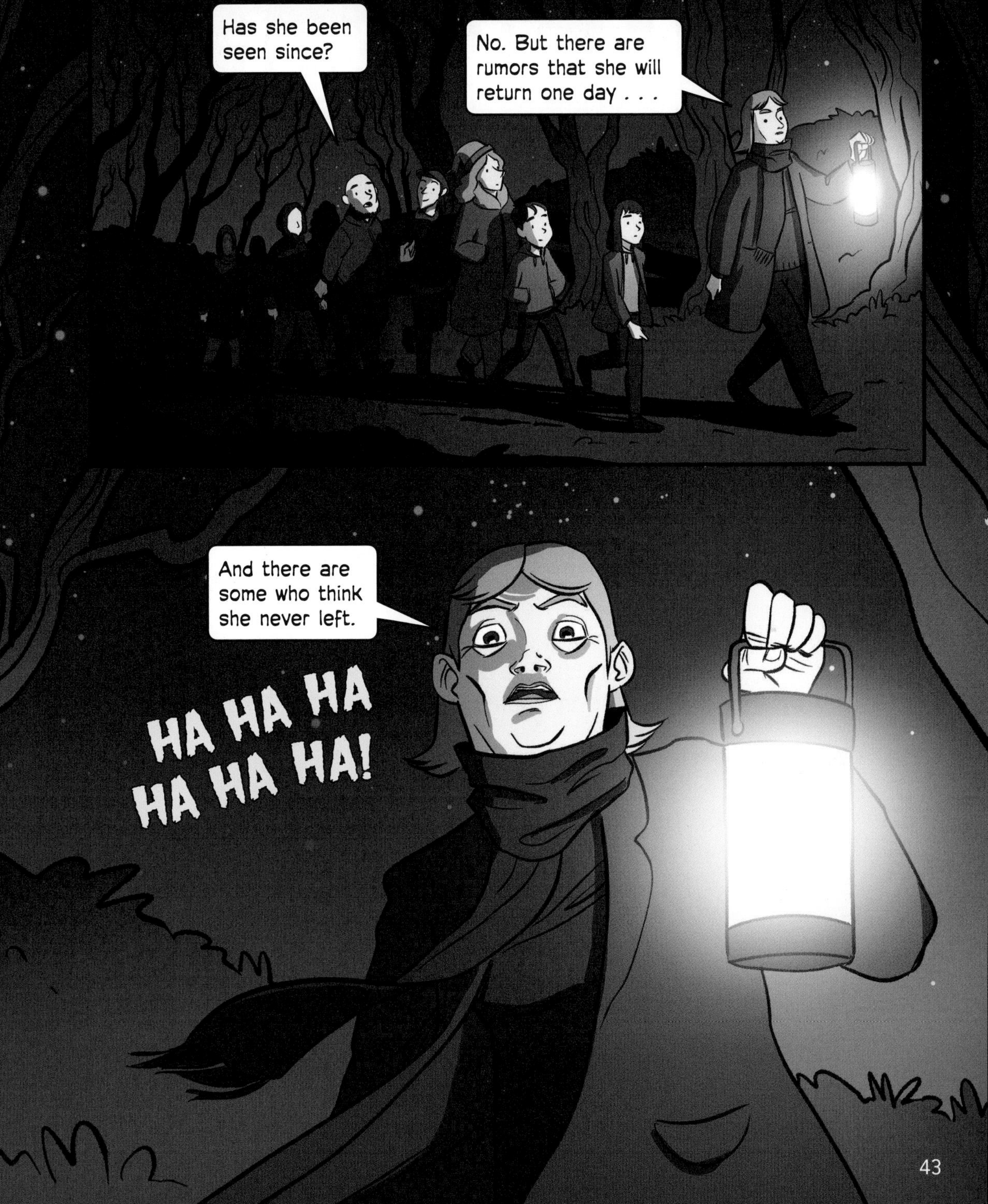
Has she been seen since?
No. But there are rumors that she will return one day . . .
And there are some who think she never left.
HA HA HA HA HA HA!

MORE ABOUT THE
BELL WITCH GHOST

- Much of what we know about the Bell Witch comes from *An Authentic History of the Famous Bell Witch* written by M. V. Ingram. Ingram was a newspaper editor from Tennessee.

- Ingram claimed he had Richard William Bell's journal, *Our Family Trouble: The Story of the Bell Witch of Tennessee.* Richard was one of John and Lucy's youngest children. But there is no proof that his journal ever existed.

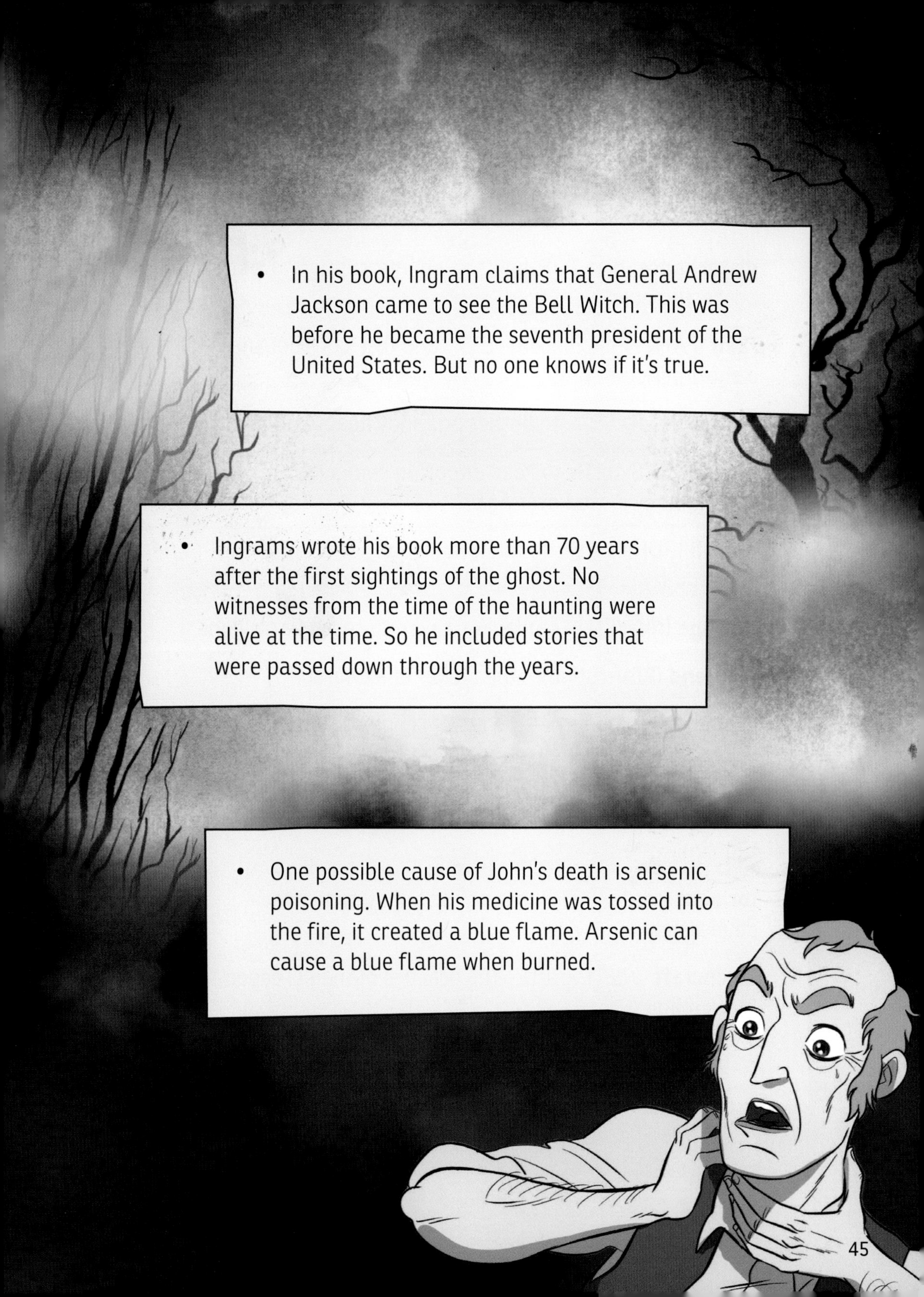
• In his book, Ingram claims that General Andrew Jackson came to see the Bell Witch. This was before he became the seventh president of the United States. But no one knows if it's true.
• Ingrams wrote his book more than 70 years after the first sightings of the ghost. No witnesses from the time of the haunting were alive at the time. So he included stories that were passed down through the years.
• One possible cause of John's death is arsenic poisoning. When his medicine was tossed into the fire, it created a blue flame. Arsenic can cause a blue flame when burned.

GLOSSARY

disturbance (diss-TUR-bents)—an interruption to a state of peace and quiet

faint (FAYNT)—to become dizzy and lose consciousness for a short period of time

harass (ha-RASS)—to bother or annoy again and again

pester (PESS-tur)—to keep annoying someone by doing something over and over again

punish (PUHN-ish)—to make someone suffer for doing something wrong

revenge (rih-VENJ)—an action taken to repay harm done

reverend (REV-ruhnd)—the leader of a church

secrecy (SEE-kri-see)—the act of keeping something hidden

spirit (SPIHR-it)—a ghost

theory (THEE-ur-ee)—an idea that explains something that is unknown

torment (tor-MENT)—to upset or annoy someone deliberately

witchcraft (WICH-kraft)—the practice of magic, especially black magic

READ MORE

Andrews, Elizabeth. *Haunted Places*. Minneapolis: Pop!, 2022.

Katz, Susan. *Famous Ghosts*. Minneapolis: Lerner Publications, 2024.

Peterson, Megan Cooley. *The Bell Witch: An American Ghost Story*. North Mankato, MN: Capstone Press, 2020.

INTERNET SITES

Historic Bell Witch Cave
bellwitchcave.com

Mental Floss: The Spookiest Ghost Stories from All 50 States
mentalfloss.com/article/504950/spookiest-ghost-stories-all-50-states

Tennessee Myths and Legends
sharetngov.tnsosfiles.com/tsla/exhibits/myth/bellwitch.htm

ABOUT THE AUTHOR

Photo by Russell Griesmer

Blake A. Hoena grew up in central Wisconsin, where he wrote stories about robots conquering the moon and trolls lumbering around the woods behind his parents' house. He now lives in Minnesota and enjoys writing about fun things like history, space aliens, cryptids, and superheroes. Blake has written more than fifty chapter books and dozens of graphic novels for children.

ABOUT THE ILLUSTRATOR

Photo by
Francesco Pischetola

Long ago, **Amerigo Pinelli** met a pencil when he was a child living in the heart of the city of Naples, Italy. From that moment on he started to play, joke, fight, and make peace with it. Today, he works in animation and publishing, and he also teaches kids in the comics school of Naples. He thinks making a living doing the thing he enjoys the most is a great gift, and he considers himself very lucky. His three daughters Chiara, Teresa, and Irene fill his life with color and joy. They are really unpredictable! For him and his wife, Giulia, it's impossible to get bored!